W9-DBE-060

ONE NATION AGAIN

A SOURCEBOOK ON THE CIVIL WAR

EMANC

ONE NATION AGAIN

A SOURCEBOOK ON THE CIVIL WAR

Edited by Carter Smith

AMERICAN ALBUMS FROM THE COLLECTIONS OF
THE LIBRARY OF CONGRESS

THE MILLBROOK PRESS, *Brookfield, Connecticut*

Cover: "The Fifteenth Amendment, Celebrated May 19th, 1870." Original design
   by James C. Beard, 1870.

Title Page: "Emancipation." Engraving by Thomas Nast, 1865.

Contents Page: "The Soldier's Record: 39th Regiment, Company G, Mass.
   Volunteers." Lithograph by Currier & Ives, 1862.

Back Cover: Reconstruction tobacco label, 1868.

Library of Congress Cataloging-in-Publication Data

One nation again : a sourcebook on the Civil War / edited by Carter Smith.
      p. cm. — (American albums from the collections of the Library of
Congress)
      Includes bibliographical references and index.
      Summary: Uses a variety of contemporary materials to describe and
illustrate key events during the Reconstruction period that followed the Civil
War.
      ISBN 1-56294-266-2 (lib. bdg.) ISBN 1-56294-883-0 (pbk.)
      1. Reconstruction—Juvenile literature. 2. Reconstruction—Pictorial
works—Juvenile literature. 3. Reconstruction—Sources—Juvenile literature.
4. United States—Politics and government—1865–1877—Juvenile literature.
5. United States—Politics and government—1865–1877—Pictorial works—
Juvenile literature. 6. United States—Politics and government—1865–1877—
Sources—Juvenile literature. [1. Reconstruction—Sources. 2. United States—
Politics and government—1865–1877—Sources.] I. Smith, C. Carter.
II. Series.
E668.O54 1993
973.8'1'0222—dc20   92-16661
                                                                        CIP
                                                                        AC

 Created in association with Media Projects Incorporated

C. Carter Smith, *Executive Editor*
Lelia Wardwell, *Managing Editor*
Charles A. Wills, *Principal Writer*
Kimberly Horstman, *Picture and Production Editor*
Lydia Link, *Designer*
Athena Angelos, *Photo Researcher*

The consultation of Bernard F. Reilly, Jr., Head Curator of the Prints and
Photographs Division of the Library of Congress, is gratefully acknowledged.

Contents

A returning Union soldier is reunited with his wife and child in this Currier & Ives lithograph titled "Home from the War." There would be no such happy scenes for the families of the more than 600,000 Northern and Southern soldiers and sailors who died in the Civil War.

Introduction

ONE NATION AGAIN is one of the volumes in a series published by The Millbrook Press titled AMERICAN ALBUMS FROM THE COLLECTIONS OF THE LIBRARY OF CONGRESS, and one of six books in the series subtitled SOURCEBOOKS ON THE CIVIL WAR.

The editors' basic goal for the series is to make available to the student many of the original visual documents preserved in the Library of Congress as records of the American past. The volumes in THE CIVIL WAR series reproduce prints, maps, paintings, and other works in the Library's special collections divisions, and a few from its general book collections. Most prominently featured in this series are the holdings of the Prints and Photographs Division.

The end of the war and Lincoln's assassination launched an almost national cult of adoration for the president, expressed in mourning and memorial prints, allegories, and photographs of his birthplace and other shrines. In some prints, Lincoln was even equated with such awe-inspiring figures as George Washington. What made this admiration all the more remarkable was that it was quite a shift from the controversial image that Lincoln experienced during most of his presidency.

With Lincoln a martyr, Northern cartoonists soon turned their talents to ridiculing former Confederate president Jefferson Davis. Countless cartoons exaggerated the circumstances under which Davis was captured by Union troops. The beginnings of the long tradition of reformist political cartooning began during this period in Northern journals such as *Harper's Weekly*. At first these glorified the war, in retrospect, as a crusade against slavery and presented a utopian vision of racial harmony and freedmen's rights. The optimistic vision concocted by artists like Thomas Nast soon evaporated in the face of the erosion, under the Johnson administration, of the civil rights advances made by Reconstruction policies. And the artists' commentaries in these same newspapers were harshly opposed to the Johnson and, later, Grant administrations.

The documents reproduced here represent a small but telling portion of the rich pictorial record of the Civil War preserved by the Library of Congress in its role as the nation's library.

BERNARD F. REILLY, JR.

The United States continued to grow during the Civil War and Reconstruction. West Virginia, created from Virginia's pro-Union western counties, became a state in 1863. Nevada was admitted to the Union in October 1864; its state motto, "born of battle," honors its wartime statehood. By the time Reconstruction ended in 1877, two more states—Nebraska and Colorado—had joined the Union, bringing the total to thirty-seven.

The nation's major territorial gain during Reconstruction, the Alaska Purchase, nearly fell through because of the bitter political battles of the era. In 1866, Russia offered to sell the vast Alaska Territory—a region twice as large as Texas—to the United States. Secretary of State William Seward offered $5 million, but the final price agreed upon by both countries was $7.2 million. By the time Seward drafted a treaty authorizing the purchase, however, the Senate (which had to ratify it) had adjourned for the year. President Andrew Johnson called the Senate back for a special session. At first, many senators opposed the purchase—not because they thought buying Alaska was a bad idea, but because there was already such animosity between Johnson and Congress over how to reconstruct the nation. But on April 9, 1867, the Senate ratified the treaty.

The treaty then went to the House of Representatives, which had to approve the money for the purchase. For more than a year the House refused to do so. Finally, after a campaign that included bribes to several influential representatives, Congress voted to approve the purchase on July 14, 1868.

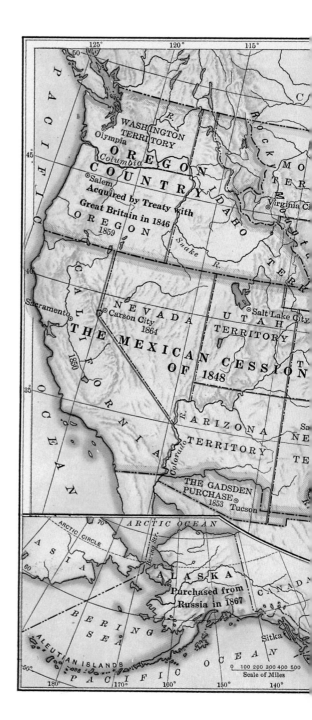

THE GROWTH
of the
UNITED STATES
From 1776 to 1867

The acquisitions made by the United States from
1776 to 1867 are shown by different colors.

The boundaries of the States and Territories at the close
of 1867 are outlined by solid green lines:

The Capitals of the States and Territories
in 1867 are shown on map by: ⊙

Scale of Miles
0   100   200   400   600

THE M.-N. WORKS.

9

A TIMELINE OF MAJOR EVENTS
1865–1867

WORLD HISTORY

1865 A dispute between the South American nations of Brazil and Uruguay escalates into a major war. Eventually, Brazil, Argentina, and Uruguay form an alliance against Paraguay.

1866 Prussia, the most powerful of the several German states, declares war on Austria. The war ends in a quick victory for Prussia.
•A ship carrying slaves to Cuba is forced to return its human cargo to their West African homeland. Pressure from Central and South American governments, as

Cuban slave ship

well as the Union victory in the American Civil War, is fast ending what is left of the slave trade.
•Swedish inventor Alfred Nobel develops dynamite, an explosive.

1867 Britain grants Canada self-governing status in every matter except foreign policy.

AMERICAN HISTORY AND CULTURE

April 14, 1865 President Lincoln is shot by John Wilkes Booth. He dies early the next morning, and Andrew Johnson is made president.

1866 Sioux Indians attack U.S. Army posts along the Bozeman Trail in the Montana Territory, beginning the two-year conflict called Red Cloud's War.

May 10 Supporters of women's rights hold a convention in New York City and organize the American Equal Rights Association.

Their chief goal is to win the vote for American women.

December A cholera epidemic sweeps the nation, killing 50,000 people.

1867 Nebraska becomes the 37th state.
•Horatio Alger publishes *Ragged Dick*, the first in a series

of popular novels that promote the virtues of hard work and clean, honest living.

April 9 By one vote, the Senate ratifies Secretary of State William Seward's $7.2 million purchase of Alaska from Russia. Many people view the purchase as a

RECONSTRUCTION

May 10, 1865 Confederate president Jefferson Davis is captured by Union troops near Irwinville, Georgia.

July 27 Four of the people convicted in the plot to assassinate Lincoln are hanged in Washington.

November The Confederate warship *Shenandoah*, which had continued to capture and burn Northern ships after the war's end, finally surrenders to

British authorities at Liverpool.

December Radical Republicans, angry with President Johnson's lenient Reconstruction policies, set up the Joint Committee on Reconstruction.

1866 Confederate veterans organize

the Ku Klux Klan, which is made up of several white supremacist secret societies.

April Congress passes the Civil Rights Bill of 1866, which forbids states to discriminate on the basis of race.

•A successful rebellion led by Benito Juarez topples the French-installed government of Emperor Maximilian in Mexico. Maximilian is executed on June 19.

•Austria and Hungary agree to unite under one ruler, Emperor Franz Josef of the Hapsburg dynasty. The new empire includes much of Eastern Europe.

•Scottish surgeon Joseph Lister, convinced that cleanliness of hospitals and surgical instruments reduces the threat of infection, publishes his findings.

•The first volume of Karl Marx's *Das Kapital* (*Capital*) is published in London. The book expresses Marx's belief that workers must unite to seize control of industry or else be exploited by its owners.

•British troops invade Ethiopia, one of Africa's few independent nations, to free British hostages. The British defeat Ethiopia's Emperor Tewodros (Theodore) in a battle on April 13.

•Fenians—Irish patriots determined to free Ireland from British rule—explode bombs in London and Manchester, England, killing a dozen people.

---

waste and call the new territory "Seward's Folly."

June Christopher Sholes of Connecticut is granted a patent for the first truly functional typewriter.

September 5 The first herd of Texas cattle arrives in Abilene, Kansas, for shipment to Chicago by rail, beginning the era of great cattle drives in the West.

December "Commodore" Cornelius Vanderbilt takes control of the New York Central Railroad by manipulating the company's stock.

Cattle drive in the West

May Forty-six people die in race riots in Memphis, Tennessee.

June The Fourteenth Amendment is passed by Congress. It states that all persons born in the United States are entitled to full rights as citizens.

November Union veterans establish the Grand Army of the Republic, which favors Republican policies and candidates.

1867 Alabama refuses to ratify the Fourteenth Amendment; Congress replaces the elected state government with military rule.

March Congress passes the first Reconstruction Act, which puts former Confederate states under military government.

May Former Confederate president Jefferson Davis is freed from prison.

July 19 Congress passes a second Reconstruction Act; this allows the South's military governments to decide who is eligible to vote.

A TIMELINE OF MAJOR EVENTS
1868–1870

WORLD HISTORY

1868 A group of reform-minded Japanese nobles overthrows Japan's ruler, the shogun, and installs the sixteen-year-old Emperor Meiji in his place.
•Military officers in Spain rebel and bring down the government of Queen Isabella. A new constitution, granting freedom of the press and other liberal reforms, is proclaimed in 1869.
•The Trades Union Congress, later Britain's largest labor organization, is founded.

1869 Paraguay's capital, Asuncion, is captured by Brazilian, Argentinean, and Uruguayan forces, ending a four-year war which has caused the death of two-thirds of Paraguay's population.
•Russian scientist Dmitri Mendeleyev invents the Periodic Table for the earth's chemical elements.
•British philosopher John Stuart Mill publishes *The Subjection of Women*. The book (inspired largely by the thoughts of his wife, Harriet) lends support to the growing British women's rights movement.
•Metis—Canadians of French and Indian ancestry—launch a rebellion in the nation's western region.

AMERICAN HISTORY AND CULTURE

July, 1868 Congress organizes the Wyoming Territory.

November 6 The Fort Laramie Treaty is signed by Sioux leaders, ending Red Cloud's War. In a rare Indian victory, the U.S. Army agrees to abandon forts in Sioux territory, on the Bozeman Trail.

November 27 The U.S. 7th Cavalry—commanded by Civil War hero George Custer—attacks a camp of Cheyenne Indians along the Washita River, in what is now Oklahoma.

General George Custer

1869 The Wyoming Territory grants women the vote—the first state or territory to do so.
•George Westinghouse patents the air brake, which greatly improves the safety of railroad travel.
•The first professional baseball team—the Cincinnati Red

RECONSTRUCTION

February 1868 President Andrew Johnson fires Secretary of War Edwin Stanton. The angry Radical Republican controlled Congress votes to impeach Johnson for "high crimes and misdemeanors."

May Johnson's impeachment trial ends in acquittal.

June Seven former Confederate states are readmitted to the Union.

July 28 The Fourteenth Amendment becomes law after having been ratified by all the states.

November Former Union commander Ulysses S. Grant defeats Democrat Horatio Seymour in the presidential election.

January, 1869 The National Convention of Colored Men is organized in Washington. The organization, which aims to protect the right to vote and promote education for blacks, elects Frederick Douglass as its first president.

February Congress adopts the Fifteenth Amendment

•The Suez Canal is opened after ten years of construction. The canal, built largely with French money, connects the Mediterranean and Red seas, and reduces travel time between Europe and east Asia by weeks.
•The Vatican Council opens under the leader-ship of Pope Pius IX. The Council, the first such meeting in three centuries, later declares the Pope to be infallible (without error) when speaking on Church matters.

1870 Prussia's prime minister Otto von Bismarck releases the "Ems Dispatch"—a tele-graph message to Prussian Kaiser (King) Wilhelm. The telegraph is worded in a way that is insulting to France.

Pope Pius IX

France declares war on Prussia on July 19. Less than six weeks later, Prussian troops overwhelm forces led by French emperor Louis Napoleon at Sedan. The Prussians then surround Paris and begin a siege of the French capital.
•Rome becomes the capital of Italy.

Stockings—is organized.

May 10 The last spike of the transcontinental railroad is driven in near Promontory Point, Utah Territory.

December The Knights of Labor is founded in Phila-delphia. The group becomes the na-tion's largest and most influential labor organization, with a membership of 700,000 by 1886.

1870 The popula-tion of the United States reaches 39.8 million.

January 10 Brothers John and William Rockefeller found the Standard Oil Company of Ohio. Standard Oil becomes the nation's leading petroleum refiner and the foundation of a vast financial empire.

July 24 The first passenger train from San Francisco arrives in New York via the newly-com-pleted transconti-nental railroad.

September 6 Louisa Swain of Laramie, Wyoming Territory, becomes the first American woman to cast a vote in a state election.

to the Constitution, which forbids states to deny the right to vote on the basis of color or "previous condition of servitude" (meaning slavery).

December The first black labor organi-zation—the Colored National Labor Union—is founded.

May 1870 Congress bolsters the Fifteenth Amend-ment by passing the so-called "Force Bill," which is aimed at prevent-ing the Ku Klux Klan from keeping blacks away from polling centers.

December The United States' first black congress-men—Senator Hiram Revels of Mississippi and Representative Joseph Rainey of South Carolina—take their seats in Congress.
•For the first time in ten years, all the states are repre-sented in the U.S. Congress.

Klan members in costume

A TIMELINE OF MAJOR EVENTS
1871–1873

WORLD HISTORY

1871 On January 18, at Versailles, France, German statesman Otto von Bismarck declares the German states united into one nation under Prussian leadership. The ruler of the new nation will be Kaiser Wilhelm; Bismarck becomes chancellor.

•A radical government, the Commune, takes power in besieged Paris. In July, troops loyal to the French government retake the city and slaughter thousands of "communards."
•France and Germany sign a peace treaty on

Otto von Bismark

May 10. Under its terms, France cedes the provinces of Alsace and Lorraine to Germany.

AMERICAN HISTORY AND CULTURE

1871 The National Rifle Association is founded by former Union general Ambrose Burnside.

March 3 President Grant establishes the Civil Service Commission to ensure fairness in hiring for federal jobs.

October 8-11 A huge fire sweeps Chicago, destroying much of the city. Property damages reach almost $200 million.

November 10 American journalist Henry M. Stanley finds the "lost" Scottish missionary and explorer Dr. David Livingston near Lake Tanganyika in Central Africa.

December Reformers finally topple the empire of William Marcy "Boss" Tweed, corrupt political boss of New York City. Tweed and his associates have

been responsible for draining millions of dollars from the city's treasury.

1872 Nineteen people die in a riot against Chinese immigrants in Los Angeles, California. Congress later restricts immigration in response to fears of economic competition from

RECONSTRUCTION

March, 1871 Military government ends in Georgia after the state legislature ratifies the Fifteenth Amendment. The return of the Georgia delegation to Congress greatly increases Southern strength in Congress.

April Another "Force Bill" authorizes the army to take action against the Ku Klux Klan and similar groups.

May The Treaty of Washington is signed; it calls for an international court to decide if

Britain should pay the U.S. for shipping losses caused by British-built Confederate warships. In September, Britain agrees to pay the U.S. $15 million.

March, 1872 Over 500 suspected Klan members are arrested by federal

authorities; fifty-five are eventually convicted.

May A group of moderate Republicans breaks away to form the Liberal Republican Party, which nominates Horace Greeley for president. Greeley, who is also endorsed by the

•King Victor Emmanuelle II of Italy guarantees the Vatican the status of an independent state.

1872 Czar Alexander of Russia, Kaiser Wilhelm of Germany, and Emperor Franz Josef of Austria form an alliance called, in German, the Dreikaiserbund (League of Three Emperors). The alliance hopes to keep the peace in an increasingly restless Eastern Europe.
•Civil war breaks out in Spain between Carlists (supporters of King Don Carlos) and those who favor a republic.
•The British

Parliament passes the Ballot Act. The measure authorizes voting by secret ballot in national elections.

1873 Russia's conquests in Central Asia continue with the capture of Khiva, capital of Uzbekistan; Turkestan falls the following year.
•A republican

government is established in Spain but the struggle between republicans and Carlists continues with the country's military leaders favoring an overthrow of the new liberal government.

Chinese laborers.
•The first national park, Yellowstone, is established in Wyoming by Congress.
•Mormon leader Brigham Young is arrested in Salt Lake City, Utah Territory, for practicing polygamy.

October Modoc Indians in California

resist orders to return to their Oregon reservation; one of their leaders, Kintpuash ("Captain Jack" to whites) kills General E. S. Canby during negotiations.

September, 1873 Following a financial panic on Wall Street, a five-year

depression sets in. The nation's economic woes are increased by poor harvests in the West.

November Spanish authorities seize the American ship *Virginius* at Havana, Cuba. Because the *Virginius* was carrying weapons to

Cuban rebels, thirteen crewmen are executed by the Spanish. The Spanish government later apologizes for the incident, which nearly leads to war between the United States and Spain.

Democrats, faces incumbent Republican Ulysses Grant.

June The Freedmen's Bureau is closed by Congress because resistance from Southern whites has reduced its effectiveness.

November Grant is reelected to a second term as president.

April 14, 1873 A white mob attacks the mostly black community of Colfax, Louisiana. The incident is among the worst racial clashes of Reconstruction.

Marriage of a black soldier by the chaplain of the Freedmen's Bureau

A TIMELINE OF MAJOR EVENTS
1874–1877

The Suez Canal

1874 Acting for the Egyptian government, Charles Gordon becomes governor general of the Sudan in Northeast Africa and vows to end slavery.
•After two years of fighting, Britain and the Asante people of Africa's Gold Coast (now Ghana) sign a peace treaty.

Neither side has won a decisive victory in one of the few colonial wars where a European power failed to crush native forces.
•Benjamin Disraeli, leader of Great Britain's Conservative Party becomes Prime Minister for the second time.
1875 Nationalists in Macedonia and the

AMERICAN HISTORY AND CULTURE

July 1874 The first bridge across the Mississippi River is competed at St. Louis, Missouri.

August Gold is discovered in the Black Hills of the Dakota Territory. Prospectors rush into the area, which is sacred land to the Sioux Indians, and part of their territory under the terms of the Fort Laramie Treaty of 1868.

November Illinois farmer Joseph Glidden invents barbed wire. Within a few years, barbed-wire fences stretch across the West, making large-scale cattle drives more difficult.

May 1875 Another major scandal involving cheating on federal taxes for distilled liquor hits the White House. Orville Babcock, President Grant's private secretary, is among the accused.

Bell demonstrating his telephone

RECONSTRUCTION

February, 1874 Blanche K. Bruce is elected to the Senate from Mississippi. He becomes the second black U.S. senator.

November Democrats gain control of the House of Representatives following Congressional elections, signaling the beginning of the end for Republican-enforced Reconstruction.

December Seventy-five blacks are killed in rioting in Vicksburg, Mississippi.

March 1875 Congress passes the Civil Rights Bill of 1875. The law declares that blacks are entitled to equal treatment on public transportation and in other public facilities.

May 1876 The International Exposition opens in Philadelphia to celebrate the American Centennial.

June The Democrats nominate New York governor Samuel J. Tilden for president; the Republicans pick Ohio governor Rutherford B. Hayes.

Balkan regions of Bosnia-Herzegovina start a series of futile uprisings against Turkish rule.
•British prime minister Benjamin Disraeli authorizes the purchase of shares in the French-run Suez Canal. The move is necessary because the canal is now a vital link in Britain's sea route to Indian and other Asian colonies.

1876 Porfirio Diaz rises to power in Mexico, replacing Lerdo de Tejada. Diaz will rule Mexico for the next thirty-five years.
•A revolt against rule by the Ottoman (Turkish) Empire breaks out in what is now Bulgaria. Ottoman troops put down the rebellion with much bloodshed. This leads to protests by the major European powers.

1877 Britain takes control of the Transvaal, the South African republic populated mostly by the Boers, descendants of early Dutch settlers.
•Conservative Japanese samurai (warriors) rebel against the Emperor Meiji's progressive government. The uprising fails when the newly modernized Japanese army crushes the rebels, who fight with traditional weapons.

October Mary Baker Eddy publishes *Science and Health with Key to the Scriptures.* The book inspires the Christian Science movement.

1876 *The Adventures of Tom Sawyer*, by Mark Twain, is published.

March 10 Scientist Alexander Graham Bell develops a working telephone.

June 25 Angry at the white invasion of the Black Hills, Sioux and Cheyenne Indians, led by Sitting Bull and Crazy Horse, attack a force led by General George Custer along the Bighorn River in the Montana Territory. Custer and his troops are killed.

July 4 The reunited nation celebrates its centennial with a huge international exhibition in Philadelphia.

August 1 Colorado is admitted to the Union as the thirty-eighth state.

1877 Miners in western Pennsylvania form a secret society, the "Molly Maguires," to protest working conditions. Violence breaks out and ten members of the group are hanged for the murder of mine officials.

Main Exposition Building at the International Exposition

November Tilden wins a majority of the popular vote, but electoral votes are disputed because of voting irregularities in three Southern states—Florida, Louisiana, South Carolina—and Oregon.

January 1877 To resolve the deadlocked presidential election, the Southern Democrats agree to declare Hayes the winner, in return for a complete withdrawal of federal troops from the South.

April 14 President Hayes orders the remaining federal troops in Louisiana to leave, ending Reconstruction.

Part I
With Malice Toward None

Shown here is the cover to the "National Funeral March," composed to honor Abraham Lincoln. Among the many tributes to the assassinated president was this simple statement from an Illinois soldier: "The war is over, and many are lost. And now we have lost the best, the fairest, the truest man in America . . . Take him altogether, he was the best man this country ever produced."

In 1858, Abraham Lincoln, then a candidate for Illinois senator, declared his belief that the United States could not endure as "a house divided, half slave and half free." Three years later, most of the Southern states seceded to form the Confederate States of America. By the spring of 1865, after four years of civil war, the Union was restored and slavery was abolished.

The cost had been terrible. The South was devastated, with two thirds of its material wealth destroyed. About 620,000 soldiers had died, more than in all the nation's other wars combined. And among the last casualties was Abraham Lincoln, felled by an assassin's bullet in the final days of the war.

The reunited nation and its new president, Andrew Johnson, faced two difficult questions: first, how to act toward the defeated South, and second, what to do about the 4 million freed slaves? The struggle to find a satisfactory answer to these questions would be the central issue during the next twelve years, a period known as Reconstruction.

The "Radical Republicans" in Congress believed that the federal government should rule the conquered South until fair treatment and the vote for freedmen (former slaves) was assured. President Johnson took a different view. He believed that once the ex-Confederate states proved their loyalty to the Union, they should decide for themselves what rights the freedmen should have. These opposing policies soon pitted Congress and the president in a fierce struggle.

WASHINGTON IN 1865

By April 1865, the nation's capital was a very different place from what it had been four years earlier. During the Civil War, Washington was transformed into a fortress city ringed with defenses and filled with blue-clad Union troops. Inside the city, hospitals housed the soldiers who returned, wounded and sick from dozens of battles and campaigns. A dedicated corps of civilian men and women had moved to Washington to tend the suffering soldiers.

For years, the clatter and traffic of war had filled the city. "Long lines of army wagons and artillery were continually rumbling through the streets," one resident recalled. Then, in April 1865, the city echoed with the sounds of victory and celebration. On April 3, Richmond, the Confederate capital, fell to Union forces, and a 900-gun salute was fired in Washington. A week later, news of Robert E. Lee's surrender at Appomattox reached the city.

That night, a cheering crowd, led by a band, marched to the White House. Abraham Lincoln declined to make a speech—one would come tomorrow, he promised—but he had a request for the band: "Dixie," the unofficial anthem of the defeated Confederacy. "I have always thought 'Dixie' was one of the best tunes I ever heard," he told the crowd. "Our adversaries over the way attempted to appropriate it, but I insisted yesterday that we fairly captured it."

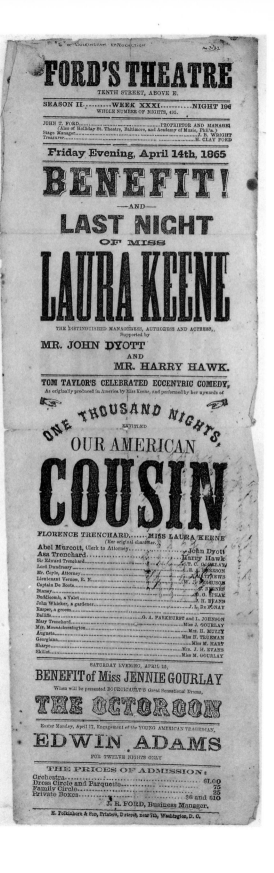

The featured play at Ford's Theatre (left) on April 14, 1865, was *Our American Cousin,* a comedy by Tom Taylor starring the famous English actress Laura Keene. Ticket sales rose when the management of Ford's Theatre announced that General and Mrs. Ulysses S. Grant would be attending the play as guests of the Lincolns. Grant was still unfamiliar to many Washingtonians, and they hoped to catch a glimpse of the victorious general during the performance.

Pre-war Washington, D.C., according to journalist Noah Brooks, "was as drowsy and grass-grown as any old New England town. The war changed that in a couple of weeks." Despite the bustle brought on by the conflict, some old customs continued. Cattle still grazed in the field in front of the Treasury Building, as shown in this photograph (below) taken in April 1865.

LINCOLN'S ASSASSINATION

On the night of April 10, a huge crowd assembled at the White House for Lincoln's promised speech. He spoke about the difficult task of reconstructing the nation. "We must," he said, "begin with, and mold from, disorganized and discordant elements." He ended by saying that he favored a proposal in Louisiana that would give the vote to black Union veterans and freed slaves who could read and write.

Among the crowd beneath the White House balcony was John Wilkes Booth, a well-known actor and an ardent supporter of the Confederacy. For months Booth and a handful of companions had been plotting against the president. That day, Booth turned to a friend and said, "That means nigger citizenship. Now, by God, I'll put him through. This is the last speech he will ever make."

At 8:30 p.m. on April 14—Good Friday—Lincoln arrived at Ford's Theatre to watch a benefit performance of the popular comedy *Our American Cousin*. The play, already in progress, stopped while the presidential party took their seats in a private box.

Shortly after 10:00, John Wilkes Booth quietly made his way to the rear of the president's box. At 10:15, he aimed a small pistol at the President and fired. Lincoln, hit in the back of the head, slumped forward.

This photograph (right) shows Box Eight in Ford's Theatre, scene of the assassination. The Lincolns, Major Henry Rathbone, and his fiancée Clara Harris were alone in the box when Booth arrived. Rathbone and his fiancée had accompanied the Lincolns to the play when Ulysses S. Grant and his wife decided not to attend.

Booth fires the fatal shot in this melodramatic lithograph by Currier & Ives (below). The assassin carried a large knife as well as a pistol, and he used it to slash Rathbone's arm when the Union officer tried to tackle Booth. John Parker, the bodyguard assigned to protect the presidential party, had left his post just as Booth crept along the corridor outside the box.

BOOTH ESCAPES

For a moment, there was stunned silence, broken by the wild screams of Mary Todd Lincoln as she realized her husband had been shot. Then Booth leapt from the president's box to the stage twelve feet below. His foot caught in a flag as he fell, and he landed heavily, fracturing his left leg. Despite his injury, Booth lurched across the stage, brandishing a knife and shouting "*Sic Temper Tyrannis!*" ("Thus always to tyrants," the state motto of Virginia). Then he hobbled into the alley outside the theater, mounted a waiting horse, and galloped off into the night.

Inside the theater, two doctors pushed their way through the confused, panicked crowd to the president's box. Army surgeon Charles Leale, a man who had seen plenty of gunshot wounds, examined the president. "His wound is mortal," he said. "It is impossible for him to recover."

The assassination of Lincoln was the keystone of a plot to bring down the entire government. Booth's fellow conspirators also planned to murder General Ulysses S. Grant, Vice President Andrew Johnson, and Secretary of State William Seward on the same night. (Booth had hoped to kill both Grant and Lincoln that night at Ford's Theatre). George Atzerodt was assigned the task of killing Johnson, but his nerve failed. Lewis Powell (called Lewis Paine) did manage to get inside Seward's house. He stabbed Seward, his son Frederick, and three other people, but all survived.

John Wilkes Booth (1838–65; above) was handsome and talented—but mentally unstable and a heavy drinker. He was a passionate supporter of the Southern cause. In early 1864, he formed a group of pro-Confederate sympathizers in Washington to plot against Lincoln. Booth originally wanted to kidnap the president and hold him hostage to win the release of Confederate prisoners of war. After Lee's surrender doomed the Confederate cause on the battlefield, Booth and his friends—mainly drifters and theater fans—switched their plan from kidnapping to murder.

A "wanted" poster (right) issued by Secretary of War Edwin Stanton offers $100,000 for the capture of John Wilkes Booth. Although there was never any doubt that Booth fired the shot that killed Lincoln, Stanton and other Northern leaders believed he had acted as the agent of a vengeful Confederate government. Stanton even thought that Jefferson Davis himself had ordered the assassination.

SURRAT.   BOOTH.   HAROLD.

War Department, Washington, April 20, 1865,

👉 $100,000 REWARD!

THE MURDERER

Of our late beloved President, Abraham Lincoln,

IS STILL AT LARGE.

$50,000 REWARD

Will be paid by this Department for his apprehension, in addition to any reward offered by Municipal Authorities or State Executives.

$25,000 REWARD

Will be paid for the apprehension of JOHN H. SURRATT, one of Booth's Accomplices.

$25,000 REWARD

Will be paid for the apprehension of David C. Harold, another of Booth's accomplices.

LIBERAL REWARDS will be paid for any information that shall conduce to the arrest of either of the above-named criminals, or their accomplices.

All persons harboring or secreting the said persons, or either of them, or aiding or assisting their concealment or escape, will be treated as accomplices in the murder of the President and the attempted assassination of the Secretary of State, and shall be subject to trial before a Military Commission and the punishment of DEATH.

Let the stain of innocent blood be removed from the land by the arrest and punishment of the murderers.

All good citizens are exhorted to aid public justice on this occasion. Every man should consider his own conscience charged with this solemn duty, and rest neither night nor day until it be accomplished.

EDWIN M. STANTON, Secretary of War.

DESCRIPTIONS.—BOOTH is Five Feet 7 or 8 inches high, slender build, high forehead, black hair, black eyes, and wears a heavy black moustache.

JOHN H. SURRAT is about 5 feet, 9 inches. Hair rather thin and dark; eyes rather light; no beard. Would weigh 145 or 150 pounds. Complexion rather pale and clear, with color in his cheeks. Wore light clothes of fine quality. Shoulders square; cheek bones rather prominent; chin narrow; ears projecting at the top; forehead rather low and square, but broad. Parts his hair on the right side; neck rather long. His lips are firmly set. A slim man.

DAVID C. HAROLD is five feet six inches high, hair dark, eyes dark, eyebrows rather heavy, full face, nose short, hand short and fleshy, feet small, instep high, round bodied, naturally quick and active, slightly closes his eyes when looking at a person.

NOTICE.—In addition to the above, State and other authorities have offered rewards amounting to almost one hundred thousand dollars, making an aggregate of about TWO HUNDRED THOUSAND DOLLARS.

THE DEATH OF LINCOLN

Soldiers carried Lincoln across Tenth Street to William Peterson's boarding house. There the dying president was laid on a bed in the room of a War Department clerk. Lincoln was still breathing, but the bullet was lodged below his right eye, making death certain.

Cabinet members and other officials filled the small room, while an anxious crowd gathered in the street outside. Mary Lincoln sat at her husband's bedside until, overcome with grief, she screamed and fainted. Hearing news of the attempt on Seward's life, Secretary of War Edwin Stanton decided that the Union capital was in danger of a massive Confederate-inspired uprising. He ordered railroad and river traffic halted, put the Union forces in the capital on alert, and called on the city's fire brigades to be ready for a wave of arson.

On April 15, as dawn broke over Washington, Dr. Albert King, one of the six physicians at Lincoln's bedside, noted that the president's breaths were now "prolonged and groaning." The end was near. At 7:22 a.m., Lincoln died. Surgeon general Joseph Barnes pulled a sheet over Lincoln's face. Looking down on the Union's fallen leader, Stanton said, "Now he belongs to the ages."

The items shown here (right) were in Abraham Lincoln's pockets on the night of his assassination. They include two pairs of eyeglasses, one broken and mended with twine; a pocketknife; a single gold button with the initial "L"; a five-dollar Confederate banknote; and several newspaper clippings. Lincoln's granddaughter gave the collection to the Library of Congress in 1937.

Lincoln's family and prominent Northern military and political leaders gather around the deathbed of the "Martyr, President Abraham Lincoln" in this lithograph by Currier & Ives (below). Lincoln's son, Robert, an officer on General Grant's staff, weeps at the foot of the bed, while First Lady Mary Lincoln and Tad, the president's other son, sob in the adjoining room.

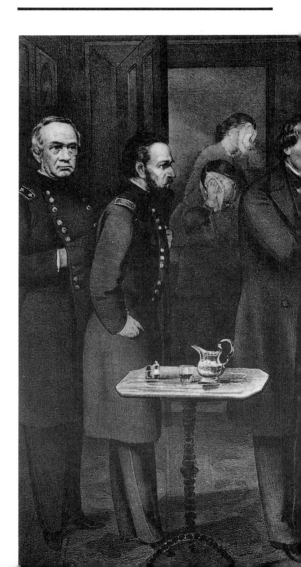

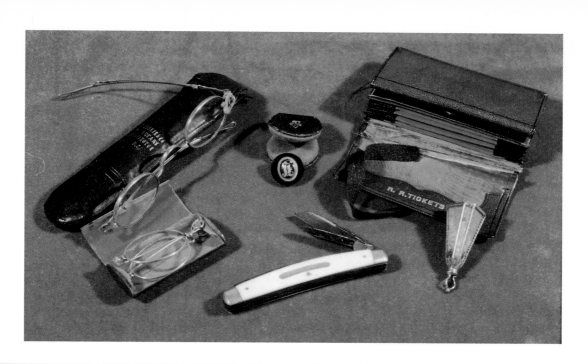

A NATION MOURNS

The president's murder sent waves of shock and sadness through the North. Despite his great wartime leadership, Lincoln hadn't been a universally popular president. But his tragic death, coming just at the moment of victory, united his critics and supporters in an outpouring of grief.

On April 19, the president's body was taken to the East Room of the White House. His widow was too grief-stricken to attend the funeral services. A long procession accompanied Lincoln's coffin to the Capitol, where the body lay in state as thousands silently passed by in tribute.

Two days later, a funeral train left Washington for Lincoln's adopted hometown of Springfield, Illinois. It bore the slain president's body, along with that of his son, Willie, who had died in 1862 at the age of eleven.

The funeral train traveled throughout the North on a roundabout 1,600-mile route, stopping in cities such as New York and Cleveland, where huge crowds paid their respects. The people of smaller communities lined the tracks in silence as the train passed. After a two-week journey, the train reached Springfield, and on May 4, 1865, Abraham Lincoln and Willie were finally laid to rest in the family plot in Oak Ridge Cemetery.

An "imposing, sad, sorrowful" procession, shown in this photograph (right), accompanied Lincoln's body from the White House to the Capitol on Wednesday, April 19. A unit of black troops led the way down Pennsylvania Avenue, and behind the hearse marched thousands of people, black and white, many weeping openly.

The funeral train (below) arrived in New York City on April 25. A crowd of 85,000 people watched as a black-draped carriage bearing the president's body made its way through the streets. Among the crowd was the poet Walt Whitman. Whitman, who had served as a volunteer nurse in Washington's military hospitals, loved and admired Abraham Lincoln. He would later write two of his finest poems, "O Captain! My Captain!" and "When Lilacs Last in the Dooryard Bloom'd," in tribute to the fallen president.

BOOTH'S CONSPIRATORS

The widespread belief that Booth and his friends were Confederate agents soon proved groundless. Booth and his fellow plotters had acted alone, and it was only through a combination of luck and poor security that they had managed to kill the president.

After the assassination, Booth and conspirator David Herold fled to Maryland, where Dr. Samuel Mudd treated Booth's broken leg. Riding on into Virginia, they hid in a barn near Port Royal, where a cavalry patrol found them on April 26. Herold surrendered; Booth remained in the barn until the troops set it on fire. He was shot down fleeing the flames and died two hours later.

Most of the other conspirators were quickly captured. They included John Suratt and his mother Mary; Samuel Arnold and Michael O'Laughlin, boyhood friends of Booth; George Atzerodt, a German immigrant; Edman Spangler, a stagehand at Ford's Theatre; and Lewis Paine (Powell), a Confederate deserter.

A military court sentenced Atzerodt, Herold, Paine, and Mary Suratt to death. The rest received prison sentences, most for life. Among those sent to prison was Dr. Mudd. The evidence linking Mudd to the crime was sketchy, and he was eventually pardoned. John Suratt fled abroad. He was arrested after returning to America in 1867, but his trial ended in a hung jury.

According to some accounts, Sergeant Boston Corbett fired the shot that mortally wounded John Wilkes Booth, but the assassin may have shot himself. He lingered for two hours before gasping his last words: "Tell my mother that I died for my country." In this wood-engraving (right), based on a sketch by an eye witness, Booth is dragged from the barn in Port Royal, Virginia, where he was shot.

On July 7, 1865, Booth's four co-conspirators were hanged in the yard of Washington's Old Penitentiary (below). The military court that tried the conspirators recommended that Mary Suratt's death sentence be changed to imprisonment. (Her main link to the assassination was that she ran the boarding house used as the conspirators' "headquarters.") President Johnson claimed that he never saw the court's recommendation for mercy, but one of the court's members said that Johnson had read the recommendation and had refused to act on it, stating, "She kept the nest that hatched the egg."

THE FATE OF JEFFERSON DAVIS

After the fall of Richmond on April 3, Jefferson Davis had moved the Confederate government to Danville, Virginia. From there, he announced that the war had merely "entered a new phase" and urged continued resistance. After Lee's surrender at Appomattox on April 9, Davis moved into North Carolina with his wife and a handful of cabinet members and advisors. When the last Confederate troops under General Joseph Johnston surrendered on April 26, Davis decided to try for Texas, where a few Confederate units still functioned.

On May 3, Judah Benjamin, Davis's secretary of state and the man often called "the brains of the Confederacy," ran off and eventually escaped to England. One week later, a Union cavalry patrol surprised the remaining fugitives—by now only Davis, his wife, his secretary, and Confederate postmaster general John Reagan—near Irwinville, Georgia. Davis tried to escape, but his wife convinced him to give up. Muttering "God's will be done," the president of the short-lived Confederate States of America surrendered himself.

Despite Northern vows to "hang Jeff Davis from a sour apple tree," the ex-president spent only two years in prison before being released on bail in 1867. Davis, who still believed in the rightness of the Southern cause, refused to apply for a federal pardon. He spent his last years at his Mississippi home writing his memoirs, *The Rise and Fall of the Confederate States*.

As this cartoon shows (above), many Northerners believed that Jefferson Davis was wearing his wife's clothes when he was captured. Actually, Davis's wife, Varina, feared her husband would catch a cold from the chilly morning air and placed her shawl around him just as the Union patrol appeared.

This lithograph (opposite, top) gives a peacetime view of Fortress Monroe, Virginia, where Davis was imprisoned. Because the government wanted to try Davis for treason, he had to be held in the place from which he "had levied war against the United States"—Virginia. It was not until 1867, however, that federal circuit courts were operating in that state, and by that time the Northern public had lost interest in revenge.

In another Northern cartoon (right), Davis is shown complaining about the rations that a black servant brings to him in prison. His guards—survivors of Andersonville and Libby Prison, two of the South's most notorious prisoner-of-war camps—reply that the food is the same that they received in captivity. Later in Davis's imprisonment, he was finally given a comfortable room where his family joined him, but for part of his early captivity he was kept in chains.

THE BOYS COME HOME: THE NORTH

At the end of the Civil War, the Union Army numbered almost a million well-armed, well-equipped soldiers. European diplomats were convinced that the government would put this impressive force to use—perhaps to throw French-supported Emperor Maximilian out of Mexico, or to invade Canada in order to punish Britain for building warships for the Confederacy.

But none of this happened, except for a small show of force on the Rio Grande River. Nearly all of the North's soldiers were volunteers and civilians, and now that their job was done, they wanted to go home.

Over 800,000 men were discharged from the Union armies within six months of the war's end. In small towns and big cities, east and west, parades and celebrations marked the return of the North's triumphant veterans. And there were prayers and tears for the 260,000 men who didn't come back.

By 1867, the U.S. Army's total strength stood at about 27,000 thousand officers and men—only 10,000 more than when the war began. Congress, eager to save money, quickly slashed the soldiers' pay to prewar levels. The handful of men who remained in the postwar Regular Army had tough tasks ahead of them: enforcing Reconstruction policies in the South, and fighting Native Americans as the reunited nation moved west.

For many Union soldiers, the first stop on the road home was a Northern hospital such as Harewood Hospital (above). Disease, wounds, and—for freed prisoners of war—malnutrition delayed the homecoming of thousands of Northern veterans.

Some of the Union Army's black troops return home in this drawing by A. R. Waud (opposite, top). According to one observer, black veterans "enjoyed wide respect and some equality of treatment and consideration throughout the North" following the Confederacy's defeat. Former Union general Benjamin Butler said that "with their bayonets . . . they unlocked the iron-barred gates of prejudice, and opened new fields of freedom, liberty, and equality of right." Unfortunately, Butler's optimism would soon prove false.

This sentimental print (right), titled "Home Again," depicts a Union officer's joyful reunion with his family. Tragically, some veterans' families were denied such scenes even though their loved ones survived the war. On April 27, 1865, the riverboat Sultana, carrying more than 2,000 newly released Union prisoners of war, exploded and sank on the Mississippi River. At least 1,200 men died in the disaster.

CARING FOR THE MAIMED

The actual figures are unknown, but at least half a million soldiers on both sides were seriously wounded during the Civil War. Many of these men returned to civilian life with permanent disabilities, including lost limbs, blindness, and recurring attacks of diseases such as malaria and tuberculosis. In 1865, the state of Mississippi spent twenty percent of its budget on artificial limbs for its veterans.

Many maimed soldiers were cared for by their families or their communities; less fortunate veterans faced poverty and misery. To improve the lot of Union veterans, Congress created the National Home for Disabled Soldiers in 1866. Based in Washington with branches in eight states, the National Home eventually maintained "Old Soldiers' Homes" in communities from Yountville, California, to Bennington, Vermont.

Another troubling legacy of the war was drug dependency. Union surgeons used morphine and other opiates as painkillers, not fully understanding the dangers of chemical addiction. As a result, many men left the service with drug habits. Morphine use among veterans was so common in parts of the North that it was labeled the "soldier's disease." Addiction was less of a problem in the South: Ill-equipped Confederate hospitals rarely offered more than ether or a slug of raw whiskey to wounded soldiers.

Dorothea Dix (1802–87; above), best known before the war for her efforts to improve treatment of the mentally ill, served as the Union's superintendent of female nurses from 1861 to 1865. She eventually supervised over 3,000 volunteer nurses.

The accurate, heavy-hitting rifles of the Civil War often caused arm and leg wounds requiring amputation. Armless and legless men were a common sight across the nation for decades to come. This poster (opposite, top) advertises a left-handed penmanship competition for Union soldiers who had lost their right arms in combat. It includes a testimonial letter from Union general Oliver Otis Howard (1830–1909), who lost his own right arm in the Peninsular Campaign of 1862.

By the end of the war, crude, makeshift hospitals had given way to cleaner, more comfortable facilities. This photograph (right) shows crippled soldiers in Washington's Armory Square Hospital. Many of the nurses and doctors who staffed Union hospitals were provided by the United States Sanitary Commission, a civilian group that helped the overworked Army Medical Department cope with the huge numbers of wounded, sick, and maimed soldiers.

EXHIBITION

OF

LEFT-HAND PENMANSHIP.

$1,000 DOLLARS IN PRIZES.

[This collection of nearly three hundred Manuscripts, written by Soldiers and Sailors who lost their right arms during the late war, was made in response to an offer of prizes for the best specimen of Left-hand Penmanship, proposed by the Editor of the "Soldiers' Friend," New York.]

COMMITTEE OF AWARD.

His Excellency R. E. FENTON,
Governor of New York,
Rev. H. W. BELLOWS,
Pres. of the U. S. San. Com.,
WM. CULLEN BRYANT,

GEORGE WILLIAM CURTIS,
WILLIAM E. DODGE, Jr.,
HOWARD POTTER,
THEODORE ROOSEVELT,
WM. OLAND BOURNE.

LETTER OF MAJOR-GENERAL O. O. HOWARD.

WAR DEPARTMENT, BUREAU OF REFUGEES, FREEDMEN AND ABANDONED LANDS,
Washington, February 27th, 1866.

REV. DR. H. W. BELLOWS—*My Dear Sir :* I am grateful to you for the kind letter just received from you, and hasten to reply. I was invited to write for the prize, but for two reasons I abstained. First, I was too deeply engrossed in my present peculiar work, and secondly, I was conscious of my inability to write a fair hand. However, my penmanship is quite as good as that formerly with the right hand.

I heard a lady in the cars lately detailing the sufferings, mortification and repinings of a young man who had lost his right arm in the service. He said at first everybody received him kindly, showed him sympathy, and gave him aid, but now it had come to be an old story, and he received no special attention and found it difficult to find a position where he could gain a livelihood.

I will say to you, my dear sir, that there are times when the deformity and inconvenience come across the mind, and disturb the equanimity of those who are full of ambition to make the best of whatever befalls. I do not believe that even the plaudits of a grateful people, or the conscious pride arising from the glorious rewards bestowed upon patriotic efforts, will be enough to sustain the one-armed man so as to make him cheerful, hopeful, and happy at all times, so as to enable him to forget all the nervous pains and sensitive feelings that constantly assail him.

My only prescription is a complete surrender of the heart to Christ.

Affectionately,

O. O. HOWARD, *Major-General.*

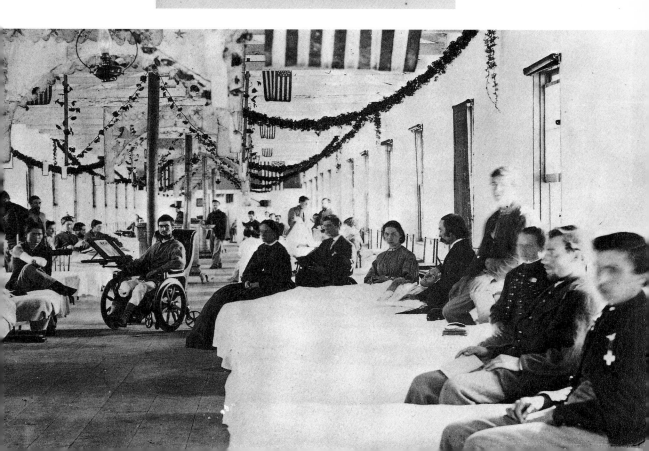

THE VETERANS

Most Union veterans returned to their homes, shops, factories, and farms. A few who had grown accustomed to military life remained in the army. Others, finding that the war had given them a taste for adventure, went West. Among these were the thousands of Irish immigrant veterans who found work building the Union Pacific's leg of the transcontinental railroad.

Most Northern veterans found ways to keep their memories of the war alive. Many volunteer units formed "regimental associations" that held annual reunions and visits to former battlefields. In the late 1870s, some of these associations began holding joint reunions with their Southern counterparts.

The first nationwide Union veterans' organization, the Grand Army of the Republic (G.A.R.), was organized in 1866 in Springfield, Illinois. Its founder, former army surgeon Benjamin Stephenson, saw the G.A.R. as a means to help the widows and orphans of fallen Union soldiers. But as the years went by and membership grew, the G.A.R. became a powerful political force, lending its support to Republican politicians and opposing Democratic candidates. (Most of the Confederate leaders had been Democrats before 1861.) "Vote as you shot" was a common G.A.R. slogan in elections following the Civil War.

Bordered by camp and battle scenes and portraits of famous Union generals (as well as Abraham Lincoln), this lithograph (right) is an unofficial "Union Soldier's Discharge Certificate." Between 1861 and 1865, about 2.5 million men had enlisted in the Union Army; another 100,000 joined the Navy and Marine Corps. Because these figures include some who enlisted more than once, the total number of men who served is probably about 2 million.

This print (below) shows a G.A.R. political parade. In return for the G.A.R.'s backing, the Republican-dominated Congress authorized generous pensions for Union veterans. By 1892, the federal government was spending $156 million each year on veterans' pensions. More than $4 billion in benefits were paid out before the death of the last Union veteran.

THE BOYS COME HOME: THE SOUTH

Union veterans came home to jubilant parades in towns and cities that had prospered during the war years. Southern soldiers returned to a society that had been torn apart by four years of fighting on its soil. Even the journey home was an ordeal for many. One Southern woman described her returning brother as "mere skin & bones from chills and fever, having walked over sixty miles and lost all save what was on his back." Gangs of "bushwhackers" roamed Southern roads—some of them Confederate deserters, others plain bandits—robbing and sometimes killing soldiers as they came back from the war.

Officers who had been wealthy planters often returned home to find their cotton fields choked with weeds and their slaves gone. One of the leading Confederate commanders, Braxton Bragg, found only ruins on his Alabama plantation: "*All, all,* was lost, except my debts," he later wrote. For a time, Bragg and his wife lived in what had been the slave quarters. The small farmers who made up the bulk of the Confederate Army often found their homesteads abandoned and their families without shelter.

In many parts of the fallen South, returning soldiers took their anger out on freed slaves, adding to a climate of violence and racial conflict that would only grow worse in the years ahead.

Although Confederate soldiers had technically committed treason against the United States, the federal government was lenient with Southern veterans. On May 29, 1865, President Johnson pardoned all those who had participated in the rebellion, except for high-ranking officers. This print (above) shows Virginia veterans taking the oath of allegiance to the United States, a requirement of Johnson's amnesty.

One out of every five white adult males in the Confederate states died as a result of the war. Malnutrition, lack of medicine, and disease caused suffering and death among the South's civilian population as well. In this lithograph (right), "The Lost Cause," a Rebel soldier returns to his wrecked homestead and weeps over the graves of his family.

UNRECONSTRUCTED REBELS

Northern leaders feared that the Confederacy would carry on a guerrilla war from the hills and swamps of the South even after its armies surrendered. Although Jefferson Davis seemed to want to continue the fight from the countryside (or from the West, if necessary) after the fall of Richmond, his generals overruled him. In his farewell address to the Army of Northern Virginia, Robert E. Lee told his men to go home peacefully. Joseph Johnston, commander of the only other significant Confederate force east of the Mississippi River, told Davis, "It would be the greatest of human crimes for us to continue the war."

Most Confederate soldiers went home and tried to make the best of their lot. Some die-hard Rebels, however, couldn't bear to live in a defeated South. Many set out for Texas or the Western territories. Others went even farther. Confederate cavalryman Joseph Shelby led 1,000 horsemen to Mexico City, where he offered his force to Emperor Maximilian as a "foreign legion." Maximilian turned him down, but about 2,000 Southerners did eventually settle in Mexico.

Another 4,000 Confederate veterans and Southern planters emigrated to Brazil, one of the few nations that still allowed slavery. Their attempt to re-create the society of the prewar South in the tropics was generally unsuccessful. Altogether, about 10,000 ex-Confederates left the country after the Civil War.

The last Confederates to surrender were the crew of the Shenandoah *(left)*, a Confederate warship that preyed on Northern merchant vessels in the Pacific Ocean. Unaware that the war had ended, the Shenandoah continued to ravage the North's whaling fleet in Alaskan waters. In June 1865, news of Lee's surrender finally came from a passing British ship. The Shenandoah's captain surrendered the vessel to British authorities in Liverpool six months later.

Throughout the war, a brutal guerrilla struggle raged in Western states and territories such as Kansas and Missouri, where the civilian populations were divided into pro-Union and pro-Confederate factions. In places, the fighting continued even after the war's end as a means of settling old grudges. This wood-engraving *(below)* shows Confederate guerrillas taking shots at a Mississippi River steamboat just after the final Confederate surrender.

PLANS FOR THE SOUTH

President Lincoln's plans for Reconstruction died with him. Lincoln had been vague about specifics ("My policy is to have no policy," he reportedly told a Northern politician), but he had made it clear that he favored a moderate approach toward the defeated South. In 1863, long before the war's end, Lincoln had proposed what was called the Ten Percent Plan. Under its terms, a Confederate state could be readmitted to the Union if ten percent of its voting population took an oath of allegiance to the Union and agreed to emancipation.

This plan was too mild for the Radical Republicans in Congress. In 1864, Congress enacted the Wade-Davis Bill, which proposed forming completely new state governments in the South and requiring a majority of voters to swear loyalty to the United States. Lincoln gave the bill a "pocket veto" by refusing to sign it. Eventually, the governments of three former Confederate states—Arkansas, Louisiana, and Tennessee—were "reconstructed" according to the Ten Percent Plan. When these new governments sent senators and representatives to Washington, however, Congress rejected their qualifications and refused to let them take their seats.

After Lincoln's assassination, the task of Reconstruction fell largely to the new president, Andrew Johnson, who was sworn in by Chief Justice Salmon Chase after Lincoln's death.

Secretary of War Edwin Stanton (1814–69; above) briefly ran the government while Andrew Johnson adjusted to Lincoln's death and his own sudden transformation from vice president to president. Stanton's high-handed actions in the aftermath of Lincoln's assassination made him many enemies, most notably William Tecumseh Sherman. When Sherman was introduced to Stanton during the Union Army's huge victory parade through Washington on May 24, 1865, he ignored the secretary, saying, "I do not care to shake hands with clerks."

In the absence of a firm Reconstruction policy, General Sherman created one of his own in negotiating the surrender of Joseph Johnston's Confederate troops in North Carolina in April 1865. The Johnston-Sherman "memorandum," the last page of which is shown here, was more of an unauthorized peace treaty between the Union and the Confederacy than a simple surrender document. Its very liberal terms were angrily rejected by Secretary of War Edwin Stanton.

Seventh: In general terms, — The war to cease: — a general amnesty so far as the Executive of the United States can command, on condition of the disbandment of the Confederate armies, the distribution of the arms, and the resumption of peaceful pursuits by the officers and men hitherto composing said armies.

— Not being fully empowered by our respective principals to fulfil these terms, we individually and officially pledge ourselves to promptly obtain the necessary authority and to carry out the above programme.

W. T. Sherman
Maj. Genl. Commg.
Army U.S. in N.C.

J. E. Johnston
General Comg.
C.S. Army in N.C.

JOHNSON AND HIS ALLIES

At first, the Radical Republicans in Congress believed Johnson was on their side. "Johnson, we have faith in you," said Senator Benjamin Wade of Ohio, one of the Radical leaders. "By the Gods, there will be no trouble in running this government now." Although Johnson was a former Democrat and a Southerner, he had served the Union cause loyally as military governor of Tennessee. The Radical Republicans also knew that Johnson hated the South's wealthy "planter class," whom he blamed for the war.

But Johnson's hatred of secession didn't translate into support for the Radicals' plans for Reconstruction—plans which by now began to include giving the vote to freed slaves. The President seemed to dislike the freedmen as much as their former masters. (Johnson, his secretary later wrote, "has at times exhibited a morbid distress and feeling against the negroes.")

Johnson revealed his Reconstruction policy on May 29, 1865. He issued two presidential proclamations. The first pardoned all Confederates—except for military officers and civilian officials of high rank, and those owning property worth more than $20,000. The second appointed a provisional governor for North Carolina, with instructions to form a new state government. This process was soon repeated for the rest of the former Confederate states. These two proclamations—neither of which fully addressed the matter of the South's 4 million freed slaves—began the two-year period known as Presidential Reconstruction.

Andrew Johnson (1808–75) was born in poverty in Raleigh, North Carolina. After his wife taught him to read and write, he moved to Greeneville, Tennessee. There he opened a tailor shop (above) and entered local politics as a Jacksonian Democrat. In 1857 he was elected to the Senate. When the war broke out four years later, he was the only Southern senator to remain in Washington and pledge himself wholeheartedly to the Union cause.

It didn't take long for the Radicals' enthusiasm for Andrew Johnson to wear thin, as this 1866 cartoon (right) by Thomas Nast shows. It caricatures Johnson as "King Andy I," his throne supported by Secretary of State William Seward (1801–72; holding back curtain) and Navy secretary Gideon Welles (1802–78; with beard), cabinet members who had been appointed by Lincoln but stayed on under Johnson. In the background, prominent antislavery activists are being beheaded on Johnson's orders.

THE END OF SLAVERY

OUTSIDE OF THE GALLERIES OF THE HOUSE OF REPRESENTATIVES DURING THE PASSAGE OF THE CIVIL RIGH

The struggle to end slavery was a long and difficult process, and it continued even after Lee's surrender in April 1865. The Emancipation Proclamation, which took effect on January 1, 1863, had declared that slaves in most of the Confederacy were now free. But the law could not truly be enforced until the Union's military victory two years later.

The Emancipation Proclamation was a wartime measure. Congress realized that it would take a Constitutional amendment to abolish slavery for good. The proposed amendment, which stated that "neither slavery nor involuntary servitude . . . shall exist within the United States," passed the Senate in April 1864, but it didn't clear the House of Representatives until 1865. After it had been ratified by three quarters of the states on December 18, 1865, the Thirteenth Amendment became the law of the land.

But the plain language of the amendment said nothing about what rights the newly freed slaves would have, or what their status in the Reconstructed South would be. "What is freedom?" asked Congressman (and later president) James Garfield, when the amendment passed the House. "Is it the bare privilege of not being chained? If this is all, then freedom is a bitter mockery, a cruel delusion."

The 1862 elections brought many Democrats to the House of Representatives. As a result, the House passed the Thirteenth Amendment by a vote of 119 to 65—a narrow margin, considering the two-thirds majority required by the Constitution. When the amendment passed on January 31, 1865, spectators cheered, as shown in this wood-engraving (above) from an issue of Harper's Weekly *that came out the following year, and many representatives "joined in the shouting . . . and wept like children."*

In this newspaper illustration (opposite, top), Washington's black community celebrates the passage of the Thirteenth Amendment with a parade. An Act of Congress had outlawed slavery in the District of Columbia on April 16, 1862.

This print by Thomas Nast (right) asks the question, "Slavery Is Dead?" It protests the fact that many of slavery's worst abuses, including whipping and forced labor as a punishment for minor crimes, persisted even after slavery was declared illegal by the Emancipation Proclamation and the Thirteenth Amendment.

THE FREEDMEN'S BUREAU

Many Northern politicians believed that the slaves would need government help in making the transition to freedom. In March 1865, Congress set up the Bureau of Refugees, Freedmen, and Abandoned Lands (usually called the Freedmen's Bureau) to "provide food, fuel, and land for refugees and freedmen from Rebel states."

In reality, the Bureau's responsibilities went much further. Beyond caring for the newly freed slaves and white refugees, the Bureau had to devise a new social order between the freedmen and their former masters, and protect them from vengeful whites. "I fear you have Hercules's task," wrote General Sherman to General O. O. Howard, the Bureau's commissioner.

Howard had few resources. The Bureau never consisted of more than 900 agents in the South, and these men and women (some of them free blacks from the Northern states) were both overworked and underpaid. In a section of South Carolina, one Bureau agent was responsible for over 40,000 ex-slaves.

Although the Bureau never had the money or the staff to carry out its mission effectively, it had some notable successes, especially in education. By 1869, the Bureau's volunteer teachers ran 3,000 schools with a total of 150,000 students. Few slaves could read or write at the war's end. But by the end of Reconstruction, thanks in part to the Bureau's efforts, the literacy rate among blacks was 20 percent; by 1910, it had climbed to 70 percent.

Born in Maine, O. O. Howard (above) was nicknamed the "Christian General" for his strong religious beliefs. Despite his efforts as Freedmen's Bureau commissioner, Howard came to believe that the individual Southern states, not the federal government, should be responsible for aiding the freed men and women.

Education was the one area in which the Bureau made a real and lasting contribution. Many of its volunteers were women from the New England states, like the teacher shown here (below). In 1869, however, Bureau-trained black teachers began to outnumber whites. The Bureau also helped found black colleges such as the Fisk and Hampton institutes in Virginia.

LAND AND THE FREEDMEN'S BUREAU

Bureau officials believed that the way to make freedmen truly independent was to give them their own land to farm. A second option was to set up a system of free labor in which blacks would work for planters in return for a fair wage.

Both plans were doomed to failure. In 1865, there were nearly a million acres of abandoned land in the South. In July 1865, General Howard issued Circular Order 13, which was to give forty acres of land to as many freedmen as possible. Most of the land in question, however, had been confiscated from planters during the war. As President Johnson pardoned more and more wealthy ex-Confederates, he gave them back their property. As a result, very few freedmen received grants for land. Some even had land taken away from them and given back to their former masters.

The "free labor" plan met a similar fate. Instead of being paid a fair wage, blacks usually had to sign contracts that gave them only a portion of a planter's crop in return for their labor. This laid the foundations for the sharecropping system—a form of economic slavery.

The role of the Freedmen's Bureau declined as hostility from Southern whites and President Johnson increased. By 1869, its functions were limited to education and aiding black Union veterans. It was officially dissolved in 1872.

The Freedmen's Bureau often had to resolve disputes between freedmen and whites because blacks could rarely get a fair trial in Southern courts. Unfortunately, the Bureau's authority was usually too limited to ensure justice. In 1866, an agent reported, "A freedman is now standing at my door, his tattered clothes bespattered with blood from his head caused by blows inflicted by a white man with a stick and we can do nothing for him." This wood-engraving (opposite, top) shows a Bureau agent in Memphis, Tennessee, taking testimony from freedmen.

General Joseph S. Fullerton addresses a church congregation at a freedmen's settlement in North Carolina in this wood-engraving (right). Like some Bureau officials, Fullerton seemed to have little sympathy for the plight of landless blacks. After taking over the Bureau's Louisiana branch, he returned 62,000 acres of freedmen's land to its white former owners. He also ordered any black citizen of New Orleans without written proof of employment to be arrested for "vagrancy."

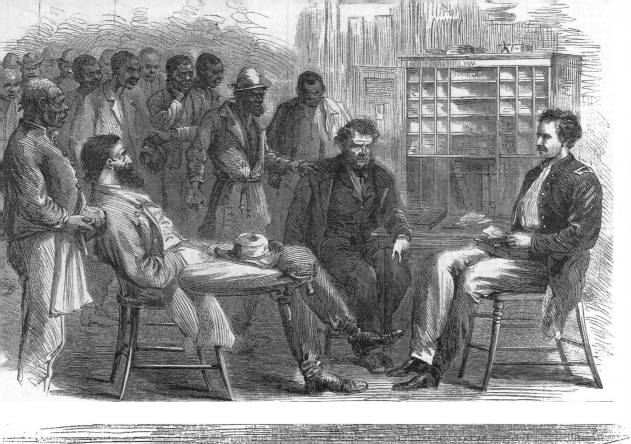

HARPER'S WEEKLY.

A JOURNAL OF CIVILIZATION.

Vol. XI.—No. 568.]   NEW YORK, SATURDAY, NOVEMBER 16, 1867.   [SINGLE COPIES TEN CENTS. $4.00 PER YEAR IN ADVANCE.

Entered according to Act of Congress, in the Year 1867, by Harper & Brothers, in the Clerk's Office of the District Court for the Southern District of New York.

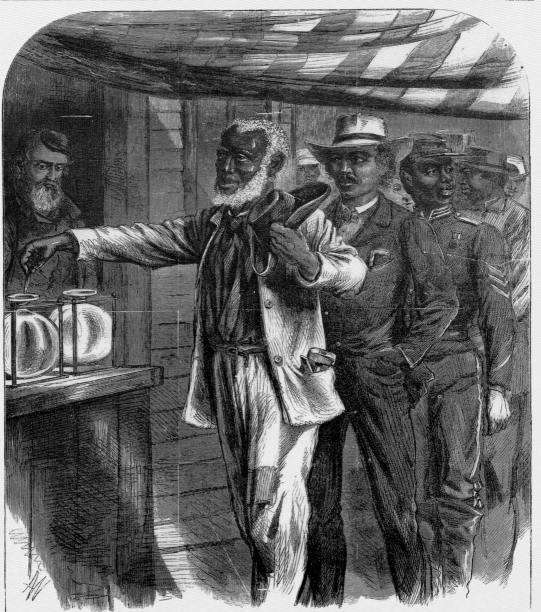

"THE FIRST VOTE."—Drawn by A. R. Waud.—[See next page.]

Part II

Reconstruction

By the middle of 1866, the battle lines for a major political struggle were drawn. On one side were President Johnson and his handful of supporters; on the other, the increasingly powerful Radical Republicans in Congress.

The Radicals soon claimed victory. Congress passed a series of laws (over Johnson's veto) that forced their version of Reconstruction on the South. The Reconstruction Act of 1867 placed the former Confederacy under military rule; the Fourteenth Amendment and the Civil Rights Act of 1866 granted citizenship and civil rights to the freedmen; and the Fifteenth Amendment guaranteed ex-slaves the vote. The Radicals had their own political motives, but they also believed that Johnson's mild policies would never achieve equality and freedom for the former slaves.

But seizing control of Reconstruction policy was not enough for the Radicals, who in 1868 tried to remove Johnson from power. The president was impeached on trumped-up charges. That same year, Ulysses S. Grant became president of the United States.

During Grant's two terms, the Radicals' power diminished and finally disappeared. Most white Southerners continued to oppose federal Reconstruction policies, and Northerners began to lose interest. In 1876, a disputed presidential election was resolved with a political deal: Republican Rutherford B. Hayes became president, on the condition that federal troops be withdrawn from the South. Reconstruction was over, and the political and social gains of Southern blacks came to an end. Almost a century would pass before the Civil Rights movement would arise and force the nation to address the issues Reconstruction had failed to resolve.

This wood-engraving from Harper's Weekly *shows freedmen—among them a Union veteran—casting their first ballots. When asked if he knew how to vote, one former slave said, "Every creature has got an instinct—the calf goes to the cow to suck, the bee to the hive . . . We'd walk fifteen miles in wartime to find out about the battle. We can walk fifteen miles and more to learn how to vote."*

DEVASTATION IN THE SOUTH

Few lands have been as devastated by war as the former Confederacy. Virginia's once-rich Shenandoah Valley was now "almost a desert," in a visitor's words. Another observer, traveling through Georgia along the same route taken by Sherman's army in 1864, wrote about seeing "a desolated land. Every village and station we stopped at presented an array of ruined walls and chimneys standing useless and solitary."

Poor harvests in 1866 and 1867 worsened the tensions between whites and freed slaves (and between whites and the federal government). "If Providence had smiled on this region in 1866, by giving it a plentiful crop," wrote a Southern planter, "injustice to the negro and the new-comer, bitterness of heart and hatred of the government would all have disappeared. In the absence of a good crop . . . all these were intensified."

Tensions were rising in Washington, too. Congress, now dominated by the Radical Republicans, became more and more dissatisfied with President Johnson's Reconstruction policies—and more and more determined to take matters into its own hands. In 1866, Congress sent two bills to the President. One called for the continuation of the Freedmen's Bureau, which had begun as a temporary organization. The second was the Civil Rights Act of 1866. Johnson vetoed both bills, but Congress overrode his vetoes. The period of Congressional Reconstruction had begun.

This photograph (above) shows blacks picking cotton during Reconstruction. By 1866, many freedmen were back on the land, working under "contracts" that gave them as little as $4 or five percent of the crop for a year's work. In the bad economic times that followed the war, banks often seized what little cotton was produced as partial payment for loans to white planters. This left the blacks who had planted, cared for, and harvested it with nothing to show for their labor.

The Freedmen's Bureau had to provide for impoverished whites as well as freed blacks during the hard times that followed the end of the war. In this hand-colored wood-engraving (opposite, top), white Alabamians receive food from a Bureau office. By the summer of 1866, the Bureau had distributed 13 million rations in the South. (A ration consisted of enough flour and sugar to feed one person for a week.)

In the aftermath of the war, some Northern businessmen invested in the South. They hoped to turn a profit from the expected rise in demand for Southern cotton, tobacco, sugar, and rice. Some even bought and operated plantations themselves. Unfortunately, the crop failures of 1866 and 1867—in addition to the racial conflict and feelings of mistrust —made quick economic recovery impossible. Shown here (right) is an advertisement for "Reconstruction Tobacco."

RECONSTRUCTION

Manufactured of
THE BEST VUELTA ABAJO
TOBACCO.

ENTERED ACCORDING TO ACT OF CONGRESS A.D. 1868 BY F. HEPPENHEIMER & CO. IN THE CLERK'S OFFICE OF THE DIST COURT FOR THE SOUTHERN DIST OF N.Y.

THE CIVIL RIGHTS ACT OF 1866

The Civil Rights Act was the first national law to define citizenship and to describe what rights a citizen was entitled to. Under its terms, "all persons born in the United States . . . without regard to any previous condition of servitude [slavery] shall have the same rights in every State and Territory." After listing the rights—among them the right to sue, to make contracts, and to own and sell property—the bill assured citizens of the "full and equal benefit of all laws." It also gave federal courts and troops the power to enforce these provisions.

Even some Republicans had reservations about such a sweeping measure. But Johnson's veto—and the harsh language he used to denounce it—swung enough congressmen to oppose the president and support the bill. The Civil Rights Act of 1866 was the first major bill to become law over a presidential veto.

But the Act said nothing about voting rights for blacks. Under the Constitution, states could determine who was qualified to vote, and the former Confederate states did everything possible to keep blacks away from the polls.

Southern whites, most of them Democrats, threatened Republican control of Congress. In the words of an ex-Confederate from Alabama, "We'll unite with the [Democratic] opposition up North, and between us we'll make a majority. Then we'll show you who's going to govern this country."

Although the Civil Rights Act did not automatically grant Southern blacks the right to vote, it brought many into the political arena for the first time. In this wood-engraving (above), a black candidate for a local office makes a speech. Most of the South's black political leaders were ministers, black veterans of the Union Army, or educated Northern blacks who went south after the war.

Outside the House of Representatives, Union veterans, free blacks, and women cheer the passage of the Civil Rights Act of 1866 (opposite, top). Although a victory for the freedmen, the law and the Constitutional amendments that followed were a disappointment to many in the women's rights movement, because they applied only to males. Several activists, including Elizabeth Cady Stanton and Susan B. Anthony, soon formed their own group—the American Woman's Suffrage Association—to lobby for a woman's right to vote.

Blacks and whites sit together on a jury in a Southern courtroom in this wood-engraving (right). By 1870, integrated juries were common in some parts of the South, especially Louisiana, and some blacks even served as lawyers or judges. One "unreconstructed" white lawyer, however, said that addressing blacks as "'gentlemen of the jury' was . . . the severest blow I ever felt."

THE FOURTEENTH AND FIFTEENTH AMENDMENTS

The Radical Republicans were angered by the continuing abuse of blacks in the South. After the war, Southern states and counties had passed scores of laws, known as the Black Codes, which restricted the rights and activities of blacks. Owning guns and gathering in groups were forbidden. Above all, the Black Codes sought to keep blacks out of politics.

Eventually, many congressmen realized that only a Constitutional amendment could safeguard the newly won rights of the freedmen. In May 1866, Congress passed the Fourteenth Amendment. Two years later, it was ratified. The amendment stated that blacks were "citizens of the United States and the state wherein they reside" and guaranteed them due process and "the equal protection of the laws." Other sections prohibited former Confederates from holding state or federal offices, and gave Congress power to enforce the amendment "by appropriate legislation."

But blacks were still denied the vote throughout the South—both by local laws and by the force of a growing number of terrorist "secret societies" like the Ku Klux Klan. Another amendment—the Fifteenth—was proposed in February 1869 and ratified the next year. It forbade states from preventing any citizen from voting because of "race, color, or previous condition of servitude."

Portraits of Abraham Lincoln, John Brown, Frederick Douglass, and other antislavery heroes decorate this print (opposite, top) celebrating the passage of the Fifteenth Amendment. Despite its provisions, Southern governments continued to find ways to keep blacks from the polls, including giving literacy tests and charging poll taxes that few blacks could afford to pay. It would take almost a century—until the Voting Rights Act of 1965—before the federal government effectively enforced the right of blacks to vote.

In this cartoon (right) protesting the Black Codes, Southern whites keep freedmen away from the ballot box. The following laws from Opelousas Parish, Louisiana, were typical of the postwar Black Codes: "No freedman shall be allowed to carry firearms, or any kind of weapons . . . No negro or freedman shall reside within the limits of the town . . . who is not in the regular service of some white person or former owner." Often blacks who violated such laws were punished by being "bound out" to white planters as unpaid laborers.

RACIAL VIOLENCE IN THE SOUTH

Violent conflicts between blacks and whites occurred in the North as well as the South during the Civil War era. Race riots swept Indianapolis and Brooklyn in 1862, and the massive New York Draft Riots a year later left over a hundred people dead.

In the postwar South, however, racial violence reached new and terrifying levels. In 1865, a Freedmen's Bureau agent in Texas reported that blacks "are frequently beaten unmercifully, and shot down like wild beasts, without any provocation."

The worst outbreaks of violence came in the spring of 1866, at the height of the congressional debate over the Fourteenth Amendment. On May 1, in Memphis, Tennessee, a fight between two carriage drivers—one black, one white—turned into a three-day riot that left about fifty people dead, all but two of them black.

Another incident took place three months later in New Orleans, just before elections for Louisiana's new constitutional convention. The city's police—most of them Confederate veterans, led by a former Confederate general—fired into a group of blacks marching in support of black candidates. Forty-eight blacks were shot dead (most of them after surrendering), and another 166 wounded. Anger at this climate of violence in the South increased support for the Fourteenth Amendment and weakened what little support remained for President Johnson's Reconstruction policies.

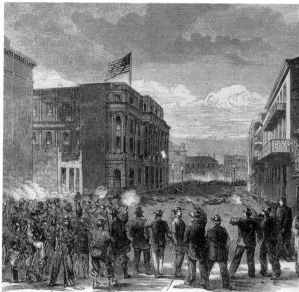

These illustrations (above) from Harper's Weekly show two views of the violence in New Orleans. A black who survived the riot testified to a congressional committee that "he saw policemen shooting poor laboring men . . . and even old men walking with sticks. They tramped upon them and mashed down their heads with their boots after they were down."

An anti-Johnson cartoon portrays the president as a Roman emperor presiding over a "massacre of the innocents"—a reference to the deaths in Memphis and New Orleans. Johnson—who believed that "radicals" had triggered the riot—refused to denounce the white authorities who had begun the violence. An influential Northern newspaper described the president's silence as "the most alarming incident in this sad affair."

THE RECONSTRUCTION ACT OF 1867

The elections of 1866 sent more Radical Republicans to Washington, a clear sign that President Johnson's Reconstruction policies were now out of favor with the Northern public. People were especially angry at the results of the constitutional conventions held in the Southern states, which brought many ex-Confederates to power.

Many Northerners wondered what the Civil War had accomplished. The Southern states were controlled by men who had served in the Confederate Congress or had commanded troops in its army. Congress's Joint Committee on Reconstruction heard terrible stories of violence and discrimination against the freed men and women of the South. And every Confederate state except Tennessee had refused to ratify the Fourteenth Amendment.

In 1867, Congress decided to start Reconstruction all over again. The First Reconstruction Act, passed in March, divided the South into five military districts, each governed by a general. Federal troops would insure that all male citizens, black and white, were allowed to vote for delegates to new state constitutional conventions.

Southern politicians denounced the Act (and three similar laws that followed) as unconstitutional, but the Supreme Court refused to hear their case. Congressional Reconstruction—or "bayonet rule," as many Southern whites angrily called it—now began in earnest.

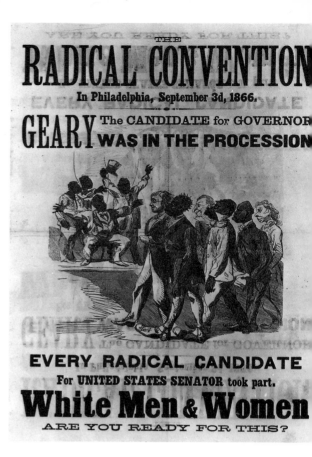

Racism wasn't limited to the South during Reconstruction. This anti-Radical Republican poster, attacking candidate John White Geary for his support of black suffrage (above), circulated during the congressional elections in the fall of 1866. Although Republican president Johnson toured the country campaigning for candidates who supported his policies, the election increased the Radicals' hold on Congress and made the Reconstruction Act of 1867 possible.

Republican artist Thomas Nast gives his view on Reconstruction in this cartoon (left). The figure on the left, a crudely stereotyped Irish immigrant, represents the Democratic Party, which was strong in the cities of the North. The center figure is a Confederate soldier. At right is a Northern banker hoping to profit from white rule in the South. Together, they trample a black Union veteran who reaches for the ballot box.

Thousands of white Northerners moved to the South after the war. Some came to organize the freed slaves politically, or to enter Southern politics themselves. Others were interested in setting up businesses. Many white Southerners despised these Yankees, who were nicknamed "carpetbaggers" because they supposedly carried their belongings south in a carpet-sided suitcase. Southern whites who helped carpetbaggers were called "scalawags." This cartoon (right) depicts journalist and former Union general Carl Schurz as a carpetbagger.

THE KU KLUX KLAN

In the South, congressional Reconstruction met with anger and renewed violence against blacks, Republicans, and anyone who urged cooperation with the federal government. Secret societies soon formed, using terror to keep freedmen from exercising their rights. These societies included the Red Shirts of South Carolina and the Knights of the White Camelia in Louisiana, but the most influential and notorious was the "invisible empire"— the Ku Klux Klan.

The Klan was founded in 1866 in Pulaski, Tennessee. At first it served as a social club, but it quickly turned to terrorism in its effort to maintain white supremacy. Dressed in white, hooded costumes, the Klan's "night riders" dragged blacks from their homes, torturing or killing those who had dared to vote or had acted "uppity," the Southern code word for refusing to be humble toward whites. As many as 20,000 people may have been murdered by the Ku Klux Klan during Reconstruction.

By 1869, Klan violence was so widespread that most Southern state governments passed anti-Klan laws. But the Klan persisted in its campaign of terror; two years later, its membership stood at 500,000 throughout the South. The power of the Klan did not begin to break until 1871–72, when Congress passed several "force bills," bringing federal troops against the organization.

Nathan Bedford Forrest (1821–77; above) served as the Klan's "Grand Dragon" from 1867 to 1869. One of the South's most brilliant generals during the Civil War, Forrest was no stranger to racial controversy. His troops were responsible for the massacre of black Union soldiers following the capture of Fort Pillow, Tennessee, in April 1864. This portrait comes from a series of trading cards included in packets of Duke cigarettes around 1900.

This cartoon (right) shows a Klansman and a white supremacist joining hands over a terrorized black family. A white Southerner wrote of blacks who resisted the Klan: "[It was] an amazing piece of heroism that the colored man should so long have taken, not merely his own life, but the lives of his little ones in his hand and have gone to the ballot-box to deposit his ballot against such fearful odds of power."

A wood-engraving from a Northern newspaper shows two Klansmen. The Klan's costume served two purposes: It disguised the wearer's identity and it terrified his victims. The most common costume, a white sheet and a hood, was supposed to convince blacks that Klansmen were the ghosts of Confederate soldiers risen from their graves to seek revenge.

JOHNSON'S IMPEACHMENT

The conflict between President Johnson and Congress reached its peak in early 1868. In February, the President fired Secretary of War Edwin Stanton, violating the Tenure of Office Act, which Congress had passed along with the Reconstruction Act of 1867. This law forbade the president from dismissing a presidential appointee (Stanton had been appointed by Lincoln) without the Senate's consent. Johnson believed that the law was unconstitutional, but the Supreme Court would not get involved. Stanton refused to leave—he even locked himself in his office for a time—although Johnson had appointed General Lorenzo Thomas to take his place.

The Radicals saw Johnson's action as a chance to remove him from office. On February 22, the House of Representatives, charging the president with "high crimes and misdemeanors in office," passed an article of impeachment. Johnson would be tried by the Senate, with Supreme Court Chief Justice Salmon Chase presiding.

The trial was a bitter debate between the leading Radicals and Johnson's lawyers. Finally, on May 16, the Senate voted to determine whether Johnson was guilty of the only serious article of impeachment—violation of the Tenure of Office Act. The tally was thirty-five for conviction, nineteen for acquittal—only one vote short of the two-thirds majority needed for conviction. Johnson remained in office for the rest of his term but did not seek reelection.

Tickets to Johnson's impeachment hearings (above) were prized items in Washington in May 1868. Most observers felt that the acquittal came not as a sign of confidence in Johnson, but out of fear that the Radicals had finally gone too far in their relentless opposition to the president's policies.

This pro-Johnson cartoon (opposite, top) is based on the duel scene from Shakespeare's Romeo and Juliet. *The three figures in the background are Senator Benjamin Wade, General Ulysses S. Grant, and Thaddeus Stevens. Because Johnson had no vice president, the temporary president of the Senate—Wade—would have become president if Johnson had been forced from office. Johnson's supporters charged that Wade, Grant, and Stevens planned to rule jointly if the impeachment was successful.*

The members of Congress's impeachment committee posed for this photograph (right) in March 1868. Pennsylvania representative Thaddeus Stevens (1792–1868; seated, second from left) led the movement for impeachment. Stevens, perhaps the most radical of the Radical Republicans, died shortly after Johnson's acquittal. He was buried in an African-American cemetery so, according to his self-written epitaph, "that I might illustrate in my death the principles I advocated through a long life—equality of Man before his Creator."

THE ELECTION OF 1868

By 1868, people were getting tired of Reconstruction and the endless political battles that went with it.

The Republicans hoped to stay in power by nominating Ulysses S. Grant, a national hero in the North. Grant, a soldier for most of his adult life, claimed he had no interest in politics. But he agreed to run, and chose Speaker of the House Schuyler Colfax as his running mate. When he accepted the nomination, Grant said, "Let us have peace."

The Democrats met in New York City in July. Their convention was split between conservatives, who favored Union war hero Winfield Scott Hancock, and the former "Peace Democrats," who had opposed the war and were now allied with white Southern Democrats. After twenty-two ballots, the convention nominated New York governor Horatio Seymour, with Francis Blair of Missouri as his running mate.

Many people expected a landslide victory for Grant because Seymour had been a weak supporter of the Union during the war. But it was a close election. Grant's majority in the popular vote was only 300,000—perhaps because violence and intimidation had kept many freedmen (almost all of whom were Republicans) from the polls.

New York lawyer George Templeton Strong wrote of Grant (above): "We know nothing of his political notions, to be sure . . . but then his integrity has never been questioned, and a man who can conduct great [military] campaigns successfully and without being even accused of flagrant blunders must possess a talent for affairs that fits him for any administrative office."

This Republican cartoon (right) portrays Grant as the "Great American Tanner." The candidate has already "tanned the hides" of the three Confederate generals at right (Robert E. Lee, John Pemberton, and Simon Bolivar Buckner, all defeated by Grant during the war) and now turns his attention to Horatio Seymour and his running mate, Francis Blair. The figure in the Indian headdress at left represents New York's Tammany Hall, the most powerful of the Democratic Party's political organizations.

Presidential historian Joseph Nathan Kane described Horatio Seymour as "perhaps the most reluctant candidate ever nominated." Seymour (right) steadfastly refused the nomination until the deadlocked Democratic Convention practically forced it on him. He went on to win only 80 electoral votes to Grant's 214 and carried only eight states, but Grant's relatively low margin of victory in the popular vote showed that the Democrats still had significant strength.

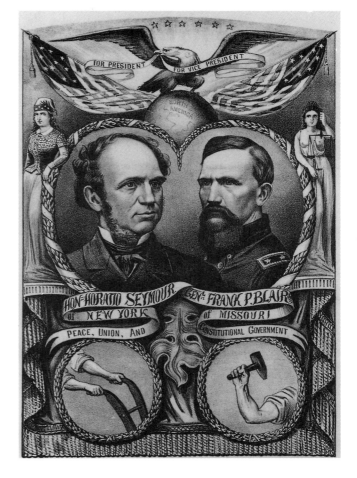

BLACKS IN CONGRESS

Southern blacks began to enter local politics soon after the war's end, despite determined opposition from whites. By 1870, as a result of the Fifteenth Amendment and the Reconstruction Acts, several blacks won federal offices as well.

Hiram Revels of Mississippi became the first black U.S. senator in 1870. Joseph Rainey and Robert Elliott, both of South Carolina, followed in the House of Representatives. Four more black congressmen—Richard Cain (South Carolina), John Roy Lynch (Mississippi), James Rapier (Alabama), and Alonzo Ransier (South Carolina)—later served in the House. Blanche Kelso Bruce of Mississippi became a U.S. senator in 1875.

Other blacks—most of them freeborn, rather than former slaves—held state offices during Reconstruction. In 1872, P.B.S. Pinchback of Louisiana became the first black governor, serving about a year after the former governor was impeached. Altogether, eighteen blacks served as lieutenant governors, state treasurers, superintendents of education, and secretaries of state between 1868 and 1877. Another 600, most of them freedmen, served as state legislators. Many more blacks were elected to local offices ranging from sheriff to tax collector.

Blacks were still under-represented in proportion to their numbers. Also, their gains in Washington proved temporary. By the early 1880s, there were no blacks in Congress. They did not return to the House until 1929, or to the Senate until 1966.

Freeborn and educated in the North, Hiram Revels (1822–1901; above) made his reputation as an official of the African Methodist Church. His "impressive and eloquent prayers" at the opening of the Mississippi state legislature in 1870 led his fellow legislators to elect him to the United States Senate—even though only 37 of the legislature's 140 members were black. Revels's Senate seat was formerly held by Jefferson Davis.

This Currier & Ives lithograph (opposite, top) shows the first blacks to serve in Congress. Although some white politicians welcomed them, the Northern press and public had varying reactions. One Illinois newspaper agonized about "semi-barbarians [making] laws to govern millions of intelligent caucasians."

The center panel of this lithograph (right) shows Representative Robert Elliott of South Carolina speaking in favor of the proposed law that eventually became the Civil Rights Act of 1875. The law was intended to guarantee blacks equal access to public facilities such as hotels and streetcars. In his speech, Elliot noted that he had been barred from a North Carolina restaurant because of his color.

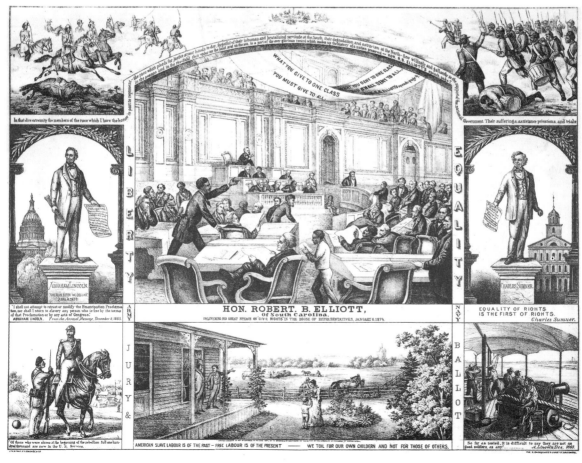

HON. ROBERT. B. ELLIOTT,
Of South Carolina.
DELIVERING HIS GREAT SPEECH ON "CIVIL RIGHTS" IN THE HOUSE OF REPRESENTATIVES, JANUARY 6, 1874.

SOUTH CAROLINA'S NEW CONSTITUTION

After the Reconstruction Act of 1867, the former Confederate states turned to the task of creating new state constitutions. By the spring of 1868, all but Texas had new constitutions in place.

The most controversial convention took place in South Carolina—the first state to secede in 1860. Because most of the state's white voters refused to vote for convention delegates, the convention included forty-eight white and seventy-six black delegates when it met in January 1868.

Among the black delegates were some of the South's best-educated and politically skilled freedmen. Although newspapers predicted a "war of the races," the black delegates worked with the white delegates to frame a constitution that would benefit all of the state's citizens, including ex-Confederates. "For us to suffer anything to be done that savors of vengeance is wrong, cruel, and unjust," said black delegate William Whipper.

The final version of the document guaranteed free public education for both races, equal access to public facilities, and suffrage for all men. (A proposal to extend the vote to women was rejected.) South Carolina's voters approved the constitution by a margin of 70,000 to 27,000—again largely because whites stayed away from the polls.

This print (above), a composite of many individual photographs, depicts black and white "radical members" of South Carolina's first Reconstruction legislature. The black legislators included Prince Rivers, a former Union Army sergeant; Jonathan Wright, a Pennsylvania-born lawyer who later became an associate justice of the state Supreme Court; and Joseph Rainey, who in 1870 became the first black to sit in the House of Representatives.

With "Liberty, Lincoln, Loyal, and League" as its motto, South Carolina's Union League worked tirelessly to register blacks to vote in the elections for delegates to the constitutional convention. In August 1867, thanks to the League's efforts, 94 percent of the state's eligible blacks were registered to vote. In this sequence of wood-engravings (below), League members celebrate Emancipation Day—the anniversary of the Emancipation Proclamation.

UNION LEADERS IN POLITICS

The generals who led the Union to victory in the Civil War were honored not only with countless poems, songs, and awards, but also with military and political offices. Service in the Union Army seemed an unofficial requirement for the presidency, at least among Republicans. Of the six presidents who served between 1877 and 1900, five were former Union officers, three of them generals. The exception was Democrat Grover Cleveland, who had hired a substitute when he was drafted to the military.

Although Ulysses S. Grant's wartime leadership won him the Republican nomination for president in 1868, many other high-ranking Union generals stayed out of politics. In 1884, the Republicans tried to draft William Tecumseh Sherman (just retired from fifteen years as general in chief of the U.S. Army) for president. Sherman replied, "I will not accept if nominated and will not serve if elected." Privately, Sherman said that the presidency "would kill any man of sensibility within a year."

Other Union commanders were elected to state and federal office. Ambrose Burnside served three terms as governor of Rhode Island and died as a senator in 1881. George McClellan was governor of New Jersey from 1878 to 1881, and William Rosecrans spent two terms in Congress as a representative from California.

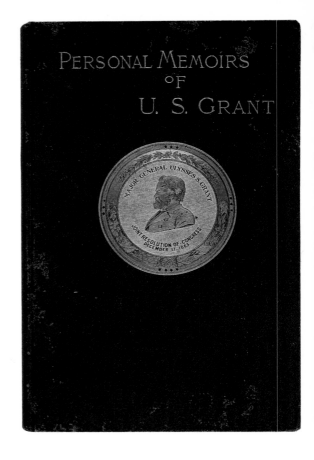

Grant worked furiously to finish his memoirs, hoping that the sale of his book would keep his family from poverty. Grant completed the manuscript just a few days before his death on July 23, 1885. Royalties from the Personal Memoirs of U. S. Grant *eventually totaled over $500,000, an enormous sum for the time. Beyond its financial success, Grant's memoirs are now considered a classic chronicle of military history.*

Ulysses S. Grant met with a great deal of bad luck after leaving the White House. He went bankrupt as a result of poor investments, then discovered he was suffering from throat cancer. He and his family moved to a small cottage in Mount McGregor, New York, where Grant began dictating his memoirs to a secretary. By the time this photograph was taken, his voice was gone, forcing him to write in longhand—a task that became painful as his cancer worsened.

CONFEDERATE LEADERS IN NATIONAL LIFE

Most white Southerners honored the Confederacy's leaders for their service in what was now romantically called "the Lost Cause." During Reconstruction, many came to believe that the North's victory was due only to its superior numbers and resources (a view most modern historians dispute). "They never whipped us, sir," said one Virginian to a Northern visitor, "unless they were four to one."

Although the Fifteenth Amendment and several federal laws barred Confederate officers from political posts, there were always loopholes. Many former Confederate politicians returned to state governments and even to Washington. Confederate vice president Alexander Stephens, for example, served in Congress as a representative from Georgia from 1873 to 1882. Nearly all of these "reconstructed" Confederates were Democrats. An exception was General James Longstreet, who was both a Republican and a friend of President Grant—and widely unpopular in the South as a result.

But as the years passed, the bond of wartime service led to more friendships between former enemies. Several ex-Confederate officers even joined the U.S. Army during the Spanish-American War of 1898, including generals Joseph Wheeler and Fitzhugh Lee, Robert E. Lee's nephew. At the Battle of Las Guasimas in Cuba, Wheeler reportedly forgot who he was fighting and shouted, "Come on, boys! We've got the damn Yankees on the run!"

Decorated with Confederate flags, this Southern print (above) gives the text of Lee's famous farewell address to the Army of Northern Virginia and a portrait of the general. Prints of Lee and other Confederate leaders would remain fixtures in many Southern households for generations.

Robert E. Lee (1807–70; right) accepted defeat with grace and courage and promoted cooperation between the victorious North and the defeated South. Although he applied for a presidential pardon in June 1865 and later swore allegiance to the United States, he received neither a pardon nor a restoration of his citizenship. The former Confederate commander in chief spent the remainder of his life as president of Washington College (now Washington and Lee) in Lexington, Virginia. This painting shows Lee in his study at the college.

Several of the Confederacy's finest generals didn't survive the war, including A. P. Hill, one of Lee's best infantry commanders, and J.E.B. Stuart, the dashing cavalry chief of the Army of Northern Virginia. The South mourned the most for brilliant, eccentric Stonewall Jackson, the general Lee called "my strong right arm." Jackson was mortally wounded at the Battle of Chancellorsville in 1863. This 1889 lithograph (below) shows a portrait of Jackson surrounded by his boyhood home.

THE DEMOCRATS RETURN

By 1871, it seemed that congressional Reconstruction had achieved its goals. All of the former Confederate states had adopted new state constitutions, approved the Fourteenth Amendment, and sent acceptable senators and representatives to Congress. Thanks to black suffrage, most of the new state governments were solidly Republican. The Ku Klux Klan had been driven underground.

But beneath the surface, bitterness, resentment, and violence still gripped the South. White Southerners claimed that the new state governments were dishonest and incompetent, proving that blacks weren't fit to be involved in politics. Some of the Reconstruction governments were notoriously corrupt, but widespread corruption existed at all levels of American government in the 1870s, from the Grant Administration down.

In 1873, a financial slump led to hard economic times in the North, shifting attention away from the South. The Northern public began to lose interest in Reconstruction.

A new group of white Southern Democrats, often called the "Redeemers," stood ready to take advantage of this change. They hoped to win back the state governments from the Republicans. In the 1874 elections, the Democrats won majority control of the House of Representatives.

This Thomas Nast wood-engraving (right)—titled "One Vote Less"—shows a black man murdered during a political campaign. During elections for the governorship of Mississippi in November 1875, violence was so wide-spread that incumbent Republican governor Adelbert Ames requested federal troops to protect black voters from white gangs. President Grant refused, saying, "the whole public [is] tired of these annual autumnal outbreaks in the South."

Despite the diminished power of the Ku Klux Klan, white terrorist organizations continued to brutalize blacks in the early 1870s. This wood-engraving from Harper's Weekly (below) shows blacks gathering dead and wounded from the "Colfax Massacre" in southern Louisiana in April 1873. With less than 2,000 troops in the state, federal authorities found it impossible to control the white leagues that terrorized Louisiana's rural parishes.

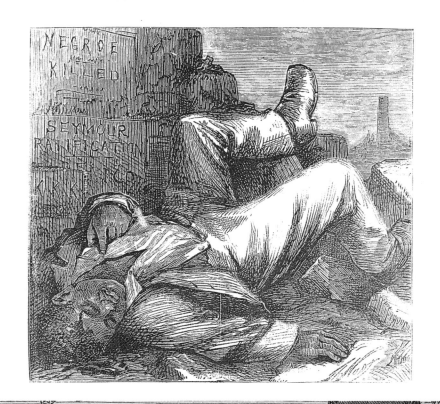

SCANDALS IN GRANT'S ADMINISTRATION

Ulysses Grant easily won reelection in 1872 over his challenger, *New York Tribune* editor Horace Greeley. Despite his victory, the president was still under attack for the widespread corruption in his administration. Although Grant himself was honest, many of the men he appointed to important positions were more interested in private gain than public service.

The most notorious scandal concerned the Crédit Mobilier of America. In 1868, this corporation, made up of major stockholders in the Union Pacific Railroad, gave out shares to several congressmen in return for legislation that favored the railroad. Among these congressmen was House Speaker Schuyler Colfax, later Grant's first vice president. When news of the scandal broke in 1872, the Republicans refused to renominate Colfax as Grant's running mate.

Another scandal that rocked the administration was the "Whiskey Ring." From 1867 to 1875, a group of Midwestern distillers bribed federal officials in order to avoid paying taxes on their product. Eventually, over 300 people were charged with participating in the scam—including Orville E. Babcock, the president's private secretary. Babcock resigned, although he was found innocent. In 1876, Secretary of War William Belknap was accused of taking bribes. These scandals discredited Grant's leadership so much that he was not nominated by the Republicans in the next presidential election.

After a hectic, divided convention, the Republican Party nominated Ohio governor and former Union general Rutherford B. Hayes (1822–93; above) for president. The Republicans sought to downplay Reconstruction issues during their convention. This led black leader Frederick Douglass to protest: "What does it all amount to if the black man, after having been made free by the letter of your law . . . is to be the subject of a slaveholder's shot-gun?"

This cartoon (right) shows Grant bowed down under the burdens of his presidency. A prominent newspaper editor wrote of him, "I think the warmest friends of Grant feel that he has failed terribly as president, not from want of honesty or desire, but from want of tact and great ignorance. It is a political position and he knows nothing of politics."

The Democratic candidate in 1876 was New York governor Samuel J. Tilden (1814–86; right), a "reform" politician with a reputation for honesty. Nominated on the first ballot at the Democratic Convention, Tilden made the corruption of Grant's presidency the focus of his campaign.

THE COMPROMISE OF 1877

The candidates in the 1876 presidential elections were Rutherford B. Hayes (Republican) and Samuel J. Tilden (Democrat). It was a close race: When the votes were counted, Tilden had beaten Hayes by about 250,000 popular votes. In the Electoral College, however, Tilden had 184 votes to Hayes's 165. In order to be elected, one of the candidates had to win 185 electoral votes. Tilden needed one more electoral vote to claim victory, while Hayes needed the remaining twenty votes.

In January 1877, the Republican-controlled Senate and the Democrat-controlled House formed a commission to break the deadlock. The Commission, made up of five senators, five representatives, and four Supreme Court justices, was supposed to be composed equally of Republicans and Democrats, with an independent justice in case of a tie. The last-minute resignation of Justice David Davis gave the Republicans a one-vote edge, however, and the commission decided in favor of Hayes. The Democrats protested, and Hayes's supporters offered a compromise: If the Democrats accepted the commission's decision, the Hayes administration would agree to withdraw the last federal troops from the South.

On March 5, 1877, Rutherford B. Hayes took the Oath of Office as the nation's nineteenth president. Within six weeks, the last federal soldiers in the former Confederacy were on their way to posts in the West.

Congressmen listen (right) as the results of the Special Election Commission's votes are announced. John Roy Lynch, a black representative from Mississippi, sensed that a deal was about to be made. "I had a suspicion," he later wrote, "that [Hayes's election] was the outgrowth of an understanding which would result in the abandonment of Southern Republicans by the national administration."

One of Hayes's first tasks as president was to resolve another disputed election—this one involving the governorship of South Carolina. Hayes awarded the post to Democrat Wade Hampton, a former Confederate general, over Republican David Chamberlain. This newspaper illustration (below) shows South Carolinians greeting Hampton as he returns to the state capital, Columbia.

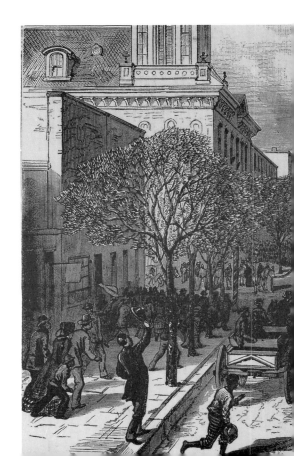

A NEW ERA

Hayes's election and the withdrawal of troops from the South ended the twelve-year period of Reconstruction. White Democrats soon won control of the Southern states, driving blacks from politics almost completely. Without federal pressure, the Fourteenth and Fifteenth Amendments were much harder to enforce. In 1883, the Supreme Court struck down the Civil Rights Act of 1875, the last major piece of Reconstruction legislation. This move led to a system of legal segregation—separation of races—that made blacks second-class citizens. This segregation endured into the 1960s.

Other changes were taking place in the United States in the aftermath of the Civil War. The industrial boom that had begun with the Civil War continued, and by the mid-1870s, the value of the nation's manufactured goods stood at three times the prewar level. Development of the West increased too, especially after the transcontinental railroad was completed in 1869.

In the summer of 1876, thousands of Americans gathered at the Centennial Exhibition in Philadelphia to celebrate the nation's one-hundredth birthday. But even in the midst of the celebration came reminders that the United States was still a nation in conflict. On July 4, 1876, exactly a century after the Declaration of Independence had declared that "all men are created equal," a white mob broke up a black celebration in Hamburg, South Carolina, killing six people.

Visitors to the Centennial Exhibition (above) marveled at new inventions, such as Alexander Graham Bell's telephone, displayed in Machinery Hall. The hall also featured the world's largest steam engine—capable of more than 1,400 horsepower—and one of the first refrigerators. The Civil War and just afterwards was a fertile era for American engineers and inventors. Between 1860 and 1870 the federal patent office granted almost 80,000 patents—two thirds of the total number issued since 1790.

Immigration swelled the populations of the nation's cities during the Civil War era. Between 1861 and 1875, almost 4.5 million people came to the United States, most of them from Western Europe. The population of New York, the nation's largest city, neared the one million mark in the late 1870s. This wood-engraving (right) shows the construction of the Brooklyn Bridge, which linked New York with Brooklyn, then an independent city. Begun in 1870, it finally opened in May 1883.

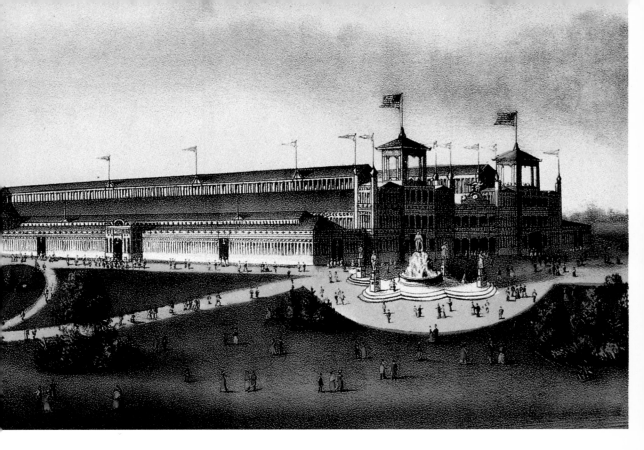

MEMORIES
OF WAR

The Civil War touched the life of virtually every American. Hundreds of thousands of families had seen loved ones go off to war, never to return. In the South, thousands of people had been uprooted from their homes; the world they had known before 1861 was gone forever. And for 4 million slaves, the war brought freedom—but this freedom carried with it struggle and frustration.

For millions of veterans, the war remained the central experience of their lives. Some felt that participation in the great conflict was worth the terror, pain, and suffering of battle. "I think that, as life is action and passion, it is required of a man that he should share the passion and action of his time at peril of being judged not to have lived," said Oliver Wendell Holmes, Jr., in 1884. He wrote of his fellow veterans, "Through our great good fortune in our youth our hearts were touched with fire."

Other veterans were more cynical. In 1879, William Tecumseh Sherman addressed the young cadets of a military school, many of whom believed that war was a glorious adventure. "War is at best barbarism," Sherman countered. "Its glory is all moonshine. It is only those who have neither fired a shot nor heard the shrieks and groans of the wounded who cry aloud for more blood, more vengeance, more desolation. War is hell."

A crippled Union veteran takes part in a parade in Moro, Oregon, in this photograph from the late 1890s (above). Memorial Day, the national holiday honoring those who gave their lives for the country, began as a day of remembrance for Union veterans. It was originally called Decoration Day, because the commander of the Grand Army of the Republic, the largest Union veterans' organization, called on members to decorate graves with flowers on May 30, 1868. Several Southern states celebrated their own Confederate Memorial Days.

In this photograph (right), titled "The Conquered Banner," a grizzled Confederate veteran contemplates a Union canteen. By the end of the nineteenth century, firms like the Detroit Publishing Company were doing a brisk business in photographs, postcards, prints, and souvenirs commemorating the war and the people who had fought in it.

Copyright 1913
by C. V. Loy

Photo by ___

THE LITERATURE OF THE CIVIL WAR

Although the Civil War made a huge impact on American life, its great influence in literature became apparent only gradually. Two of the nation's finest writers, Herman Melville and Walt Whitman, wrote about the war in their poetry. Whitman's *Drum Taps and Sequel* appeared in 1865, and Melville's *Battle Pieces and Aspects of the War* followed a year later. Both authors had fallen in popularity by the 1860s, so their Civil War writings did not become well known until the next century. The greatest Civil War novel, *The Red Badge of Courage* (1895), was written by Stephen Crane, who was born several years after the war's end.

Civil War literature is richest in personal narratives. Many of the leading military and political figures of the era wrote their memoirs, including Grant, Sherman, and Jefferson Davis. There were also countless autobiographical accounts of life in both armies. Perhaps the best known is Thomas Wentworth Higginson's *Army Life in a Black Regiment.*

In the former Confederacy, many novelists glorified the prewar South as a gracious society of happy slaves and kindly masters ruined forever by Yankee invasion and unjust Reconstruction policies. This "Moonlight and Magnolias" school, as some critics called it, lasted into this century in films such as *Birth of a Nation* (1915) and *Gone with the Wind* (1939).

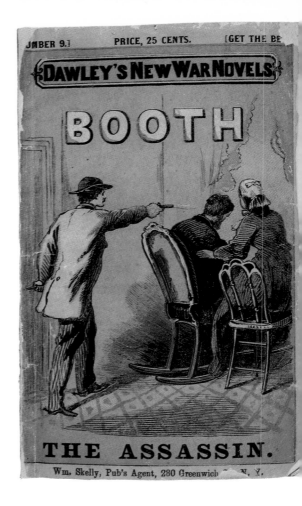

Dime novels—inexpensive works of fiction that catered to the popular taste for adventure and romance—first appeared in 1860. Most dime novels were set in the West, but the Civil War became a popular subject in the late 1860s. The book shown above is a sensationalized account of Abraham Lincoln's assassination.

The popularity of Harriet Beecher Stowe's Uncle Tom's Cabin (1852), an emotional appeal against slavery in the form of a novel, continued long after the Civil War brought emancipation. The novel was the basis for several stage plays (some of them very loose adaptations of the original text) and was translated into many languages. The cover of a Spanish edition is reproduced here.

MONUMENTS

The Civil War is still a presence on the American landscape, thanks to the many monuments built after the war. These range from huge historical sites such as Gettysburg National Military Park, which covers 30,000 acres, to the thousands of statues, plaques, and columns in small town squares and churchyards.

It wasn't until well after the war that the federal government took on the responsibility of preserving and maintaining historical Civil War sites. In 1880, Congress authorized the War Department to set aside land for preservation. The first two national battlefield monuments—Chickamauga and Chattanooga in Tennessee—were established the same year.

Private citizens also played a role in preserving the heritage of the war. In 1889, Union veterans formed the Appomattox Land Company to preserve the site of Lee's surrender, and a monument was finally built there in 1935. By then, responsibility for battlefield monuments and memorials had passed to the National Park Service.

Gettysburg National Military Park, established by Congress in 1895, was the site of veterans' reunions for decades. The last "National Encampment" was held on July 1–4, 1938, the seventy-fifth anniversary of the battle. Out of approximately 8,000 surviving Union and Confederates soldiers, 1,845 attended. Their average age was ninety-four.

Many states, towns, regimental associations, and other organizations erected their own monuments on Civil War battlefields. This photograph (above) shows the dedication of one such monument at the Bull Run battlefield at Manassas, Virginia, scene of major battles in 1861 and 1862. In the 1980s, Bull Run saw another fight—this one between those who wanted to preserve the area and the private developers who hoped to build a shopping mall on the site.

This lithograph (opposite, top) shows a widow weeping at the grave of a fallen soldier. During the war, most soldiers were buried on the battlefield, although some bought "burial insurance": In case of death, undertakers would embalm the body and send it home for burial. After the war, the bodies of thousands of soldiers were gathered from scattered field graves and reburied in national cemeteries like the ones at Arlington (Virginia), Gettysburg (Pennsylvania), and Vicksburg (Mississippi).

Civil War monuments commemorate a time when the nation was divided, but one great monument has come to symbolize a united nation spreading the light of freedom to the world—the Statue of Liberty in New York Harbor. Its French sculptor, Auguste Bartholdi, conceived the idea in 1865, but the statue wasn't completed until 1886. Its torch was finished in time to go on exhibition at the Centennial Exhibition in 1876, as this photograph (right) shows.

Key to picture positions: (T) top, (C) center, (B) bottom; and in combinations: (TL) top left, (TR) top right, (BL) bottom left, (BR) bottom right, (RC) right center, (LC) left center.

Key to picture locations within the Library of Congress collections (and where available, photo negative numbers): P - Prints and Photographs Division; R - Rare Book Division; G - General Collections; MSS - Manuscript Division; G&M - Geography Division

PICTURES IN THIS VOLUME

2–3 Emancipation, P, USZC4-1000 4–5 certificate, P 6–7 reunion, P 8–9 map, G

Timeline: 10–11 TL, ship, G; RC, cattle drive, P, USZ62-7792 12–13 LC, Custer, P; TR, Pope Pius, G; BR, Klan, P 14–15 TL, Bismark, G; BR, wedding, P 16–17 TL, canal, G; LC, telephone, G; BR, building, G

Part I: 18–19 Lincoln, P 20–21 TL, playbill, P, USZ62-32073; BR, field, P, B8184-10153 22–23 TR, theatre box, P, B8171-3403; C, assassination, P 24–25 TL, Booth, P; TR, poster, P 26–27 TR, pocket contents, P; C, death bed, P 28–29 TR, Washington, P, B8171-1273; C, New York City, P, USZC4-1425 30–31 Booth, P, USZ62-6936; C, hanging, P, USZ62-7798 32–33 TL, cartoon, P; TR, Fortress Monroe, P; BR, prison cartoon, P, USZ62-8756 34–35 TL, hospital, P; TR, black troops, P, USZ62-175; BR, Union officer, P, USZ62-680 36–37 TL, Dix, P; TR, contest, R; BR, hospital, P, B8184-13198 38–39 TR, certificate, P; C, parade, P, USZ62-3325 40–41 C, allegiance, G; BR, graves, P, USZ62-15649 42–43 TL, ship, P, USZ62-2199; C, guerrillas, G 44–45 TL, Stanton, P, USZ62-512; BR, surrender terms, G 46–47 TL, tailor shop, P, USZ62-23999; TR, cartoon, G 48–49 TL, House of Representatives, P, USZ62-33273; TR, Washington, P, USZ62-33937; BR, cartoon, P, USZ62-22084 50–51 TL, Howard, R; BR, school,

P, USZ62-8401 52–53 TR, office, P, USZ62-32013; BR, congregation, G

Part II: 54–55 voting, P 56–57 TL, cotton field, P, USZ62-22801; TR, Freedmen's Bureau; P; BR, tobacco label, P 58–59 TL, speech, P, USZ62-8461; TR, celebration, G; BR, jury, P, USZ62-38372 60–61 TR, scenes, P; BR, Black Codes, P 62–63 TL, New Orleans, P, USZ62-33271; BR, cartoon, P, USZ62-29246 64–65 TL, poster, P, USZ62-40762; TR, three men, P, USZ62-30915; BR, cartoon, P 66–67 TL, Forrest, R; TR, costumes, P, USZ62-31166; BR, cartoon, P, USZ62-18094 68–69 TL, ticket, G; TR, cartoon, P, USZ62-41221; BR, committee, P, USZ62-12110 70–71 TL, Grant, P; TR, poster, P, USZ62-7189; BR, cartoon, P, USZ62-8766 72–73 TL, Revels, P, USZC4-681; TR, Congressmen, P; BR, Elliott, P, USZ62-2247 74–75 TL, radical members, P; BR, parade, G 76–77 TL, memoirs, P; BR, Grant, P, USZ62-59082 78–79 TL, farewell address, P; TR, Jackson, P; BR, Lee, P 80–81 TR, dead man, P; C, Colfax Massacre, P 82–83 TL, Hayes, P; TR, Tilden, P; BR, cartoon, P, USZ62-29271 84–85 TR, Congress, G; C, Columbia, R 86–87 C, Machinery Hall, P; BR, bridge, G 88–89 TL, one-legged man, P; TR, veteran, P, USZ62-64127 90–91 TL, dime novel, P; BR, Spanish version, P 92–93 TL, Bull Run, P, B8171-7362; TR, grave, P; BR, torch, P, USZ62-14736

SUGGESTED READING

BLAY, JOHN S. *After the Civil War; A Pictorial Profile of America from 1865 to 1900.* New York: Bonanza Books, 1960.

CATTON, BRUCE. *The American Heritage Picture History of the Civil War.* New York: Bonanza Books, 1982.

SMITH, CARTER. *The Civil War.* New York: Facts on File, 1989.

Index

Page numbers in *italics* indicate illustrations